SELFISH, SHALLOW, AND SELF-ABSORBED

SELFISH, SHALLOW, AND SELF-ABSORBED

SIXTEEN WRITERS ON THE DECISION NOT TO HAVE KIDS

EDITED AND WITH AN INTRODUCTION BY

MEGHAN DAUM

PICADOR
NEW YORK

www.picadorusa.com
www.twitter.com/picadorusa • www.facebook.com/picadorusa
picadorbookroom.tumblr.com

Picador® is a U.S. registered trademark and is used by St. Martin's Press under license from Pan Books Limited.

For book club information, please visit www.facebook.com/picadorbookclub or e-mail marketing@picadorusa.com.

Designed by Steven Seighman

The Library of Congress Cataloging-in-Publication Data is available upon request.

ISBN 978-1-250-05293-3 (hardcover)
ISBN 978-1-250-05294-0 (e-book)

Picador books may be purchased for educational, business, or promotional use. For information on bulk purchases, please contact the Macmillan Corporate and Premium Sales Department at 1-800-221-7945, extension 5442, or write to specialmarkets@macmillan.com.

First Edition: April 2015

10 9 8 7 6 5 4 3 2

CONTENTS

INTRODUCTION

WHILE WORKING ON this book, I sometimes found myself contemplating a variation of Leo Tolstoy's famous "happy families" line from the opening of *Anna Karenina: People who want children are all alike. People who don't want children don't want them in their own ways.*

Of course, the original maxim isn't exactly true, since happy families come in all varieties, and unhappy families can be miserable in mind-numbingly predictable ways. And since most people eventually wind up becoming parents, whether by choice, circumstance, or some combination thereof, my version isn't necessarily an airtight theory either. Still, in thinking about this subject steadily over the last several years, I've come to suspect that the majority of people who have kids are driven by any of just a handful of reasons, most of them connected to old-fashioned biological imperative.

Those of us who choose not to become parents are a bit like Unitarians or nonnative Californians; we tend to arrive at our destination via our own meandering, sometimes agonizing paths. That's one of the reasons I put this anthology together. Contrary to a lot of cultural assumptions, people who opt out of parenthood (and, to be clear, this is a book about *deciding* not to have children; not being able to have them when you want them is another matter entirely) are not a monolithic group. We are neither hedonists nor ascetics. We bear no worse psychological scars from our own upbringings than most people who have kids. We do not hate children (and it still amazes me that this notion is given any credence). In fact, many of us devote quite a lot of energy to enriching the lives of other people's children, which in turn enriches our own lives. Statistically, we are more likely to give back to our communities than people who are encumbered with small children—not just because we have the time but because "giving back" often includes returning the kids to their parents at the end of the day.

To read the essays in this book is to notice that, in many ways, the common theme is that there is no common theme. Though all the authors are more than satisfied, and in some cases downright ecstatic, with their decision to forgo parenthood, no two reached that decision in quite the same way. For some, the necessary self-knowledge came after years of indecision. For others, the lack of desire to have or raise children felt hardwired from birth, almost like sexual orientation or gender identity. A few actively pursued parenthood before realizing they were chasing a dream that they'd mistaken for their own but that actually belonged to someone else—a partner, a family member, the culture at large. As Jeanne Safer so poignantly describes in her essay, she didn't really want to have a baby; she *wanted to* want to have a baby.

That line nearly took my breath away. Though I can now say (and as I wrote in the margin of Jeanne's piece), "That's exactly how I once felt!" there was a time before that when I hadn't yet reached such hindsight. Instead, I was trying very hard to talk myself into wanting something I'd always known deep down wasn't for me. Not that things wouldn't have worked out fine if those talks had ended with a baby. I had a willing husband and a supportive community of friends. There's no question that I would have loved my child with a kind of love I'd never know otherwise. But when I found my way back to my gut instincts, when I "stood in my truth" as the parlance goes today, I realized that what I wanted most of all was to find some different ways of talking about the choice not to have kids. I wanted to lift the discussion out of the familiar rhetoric, which so often pits parents against nonparents and assumes that the former are self-sacrificing and mature and the latter are overgrown teenagers living large on piles of disposable income. I wanted to show that there are just as many ways of being a nonparent as there are of being a parent. You can do it lazily and self-servingly or you can do it generously and imaginatively. You can be cool about it or you can be a jerk about it.

Typically, it's been the nonparents who have carried a reputation for being jerks. Some of that is our own doing. When *Time* magazine ran a cover story in the summer of 2013 showing a visibly self-satisfied couple lying on the beach under the headline "The Childfree Life: When Having It All Means Not Having Children," it highlighted a major misconception about the voluntarily childless: the idea that we don't want kids because we'd rather have expensive toys and vacations. Type "childfree" into an Internet search engine and you will find no end of tirades against "breeders" along with smug suggestions on the order of "I'd rather spend my money on Manolo Blahniks" and "My reason for not having kids is that Porsche in my driveway." Even the term *childfree*, which was coined as a way of distinguishing the deliberately childless from those who unwillingly or unintentionally find themselves in such circumstances, rubs some people the wrong way—after all, why should children fall into the same category as cigarette smoke or gluten?

When that *Time* article came out (the article itself, I should say, showed far more equanimity than the cover suggested), I had just begun my search for contributors to this book. The timing seemed perfect. As the subject was being chewed over in the media, it was clear that the conversation had a long way to go. Cable news hosts purported to be "shocked" at the idea that some people don't want kids (the more diplomatic were quick to add, "Not that I'm judging").

On the Internet, the standard barbs of "selfish" and "shallow" ricocheted around comment threads, even as thousands of contented nonparents expressed their gratitude that the issue was finally being talked about. One night I caught a public radio program on which a listener called in to say that choosing not to have children was a totally legitimate and commendable choice but that he personally had been so enriched by fatherhood that he couldn't help but think that nonparents were living incomplete, ultimately sad lives.

If the core message of this book is that parenthood is not—and moreover should not be—for everyone, the chief lesson of editing the book was that writing about skipping parenthood isn't for everyone either. Of the many dozens of writers I approached (all of whom had at least hinted, in their work or in interviews, that having children was never high on the agenda), very few were prepared to take on the subject. Some said that, yes, they were childless by design but lacked sufficient angst about it to have anything interesting to say. Some told me they had a lot to say but couldn't for fear of hurting certain family members. In one case, a celebrated novelist who'd apparently been known at one point as someone who never, *ever* wanted children replied to me with a photo of his infant son.

That's why the sixteen essays in this book are such gifts. Brave, thoughtful, and uncompromisingly honest, they are all tributes to the exquisite challenges of living what is commonly (and usually inadequately, though there's often no other way to say it) called an "authentic life." Frequently funny and sometimes sad, occasionally political and always personal, these essays show that there's more than one way to be a responsible, productive—and even happy—adult in the world.

The authors of these essays represent a range of generations, geographical regions, and ethnic and cultural backgrounds. Despite this diversity, they have one big thing in common: they are all professional writers. Some will say (and as Geoff Dyer cheekily insinuates in his essay) that makes for a less-than-representative sample of the general childless-by-choice population. After all, artists—especially writers—need more alone time than regular people. They crave solitude whereas many people fear it. They resign themselves to financial uncertainty whereas most people do anything they can to avoid it. Moreover, if an artist is lucky, her work becomes her legacy, thus theoretically lessening the burden of producing a child to carry it out.

I take the point. But the truth is that writers, outliers though they may be, are the ones whose job it is to write. They are the ones charged with putting the world's complications and contradictions into more universal terms. And while many contributors to this book refer to their writing lives when reflecting on their feelings about parenthood, in no case do I think anyone's choice boiled down to "writing versus children." If it were that simple, they wouldn't have much to say on the subject. Besides, the majority of writers, like the majority of nonwriters, want children and have them. For all the talk of a groundswell in "childfreedom," for all the ways in which it's crucial that society stop assuming that everyone should be a parent, people who want kids will always outnumber people who don't. And anyone but the most catastrophizing overpopulation hawk will say thank goodness for that.

There are notably more women than men here—a thirteen to three ratio, to be exact. That ratio felt to me more or less proportionate to the degree to which men devote serious thought to parenthood (at least before it happens) compared to women, who are goaded into thinking about it practically from birth. Still, I thought it was essential that the collection include male voices. Too often, this subject is framed as a women's issue. But men who are disinclined toward fatherhood must contend with their own set of prejudices; for instance, assumptions that they can't commit to a partner, that they wish to prolong adolescence indefinitely, or that they'll be intractably (and gratefully) domesticated as soon as the right partner reels them in.

The three men in this book draw from very different life experiences. Geoff Dyer is straight, married, and rather dyspeptic about children and family life. Tim Kreider is straight, single, and searching for existential mooring outside the realm of parenthood. In a bittersweet essay about fatherhood avoided by default as well as by choice, Paul Lisicky, a gay man now single after a long-term relationship, confesses, "I'd probably say yes if I ever become involved with someone who wanted to be a parent . . . though I might be saying it with the same level of commitment with which I'd say, 'Of course I'd move to Tokyo.'"

The women's stories hit just about every possible note. Some are fiercely unapologetic, such as Laura Kipnis's jeremiad against overly sentimentalized notions of motherhood and Lionel Shriver's confirmation that, yes, human populations are dwindling in the Western world, but that's still no reason to have a baby. Some revisit less-than-idyllic childhoods; Michelle Huneven writes about parents who managed to be at once indifferent and suffocating, Danielle Henderson explores the psychological fallout of her mother leaving her permanently in the care of relatives at age ten, and Sigrid Nunez recalls the harsh child-rearing styles of the urban housing projects where she was raised and her recognition, later on, that the writing life that had saved her would never lend itself to her being the kind of mother she felt it necessary to be. On the other side of the spectrum, Anna Holmes pins her ambivalence on the fact that her parents set too good an example. "I suspect that my commitment to and my delight in parenting would be so formidable that it would take precedence over anything and everything else in my life . . ." she writes. "Basically, I'm afraid of my own competence."

For a book about not having children, there are a surprising number of real and would-be pregnancies in these stories, ending in elective abortion, miscarriage, or a sudden change of heart about trying to get knocked up in the first place. For Rosemary Mahoney, the fear of future regret drove her, for a time, to shop for donor sperm and undergo fertility treatments as a single woman. Kate Christensen spent part of a difficult marriage longing for a baby, only to eventually find happiness outside the bounds of marriage and motherhood. Elliott Holt writes of a brief period of baby lust followed by a major bout with depression. Forced to take an inventory of her mental health history, she realized that the rewards of being a doting, besotted aunt far outweighed the risks of having children and being an unstable mother.

There is perhaps no more besotted an aunt than Courtney Hodell, who elegantly chronicles her gay brother's path to fatherhood and must confront the ways in which their uncommonly close relationship will be forever changed. For Pam Houston, who writes about the tyranny of the "having it all" message and the backward march of reproductive politics in the United States, it's an adored stepdaughter who taps her nurturing instincts. For Jeanne Safer, a practicing psychotherapist, the process of guiding patients to clarity and genuine insight can feel like a form of parenting. Meanwhile, M. G. Lord writes provocatively about how the effects of a childhood tragedy played out decades later when her then partner decided to adopt a potentially drug-exposed baby.

Some of these essays will no doubt enrage certain readers. Some enraged me in places, which I took as all the more reason they should be included. But all of them, without exception, left me feeling a little bit in love with their authors—and not just because those authors were handing me sizable chunks of their souls, sometimes with prose that brought me to tears. I loved them because of all the reactions they stirred in me, the one that rattled around most loudly in my brain was *It's about time*. It's about time the taboo of choosing a life other than parenthood was publicly challenged by people who've thought beyond the Porsche in the driveway or the Manolos in the closet. It's about time we stop mistaking self-knowledge for self-absorption—and realize that nobody has a monopoly on selfishness.

And so it is my great privilege to present these sixteen works. May you find them as captivating, exasperating, entertaining, and enlightening as I do.

Meghan Daum

BABES IN THE WOODS

by

Courtney Hodell

*The myth is pessimistic, while the fairy story is
optimistic, no matter how terrifyingly serious some
features of the story may be.*
—BRUNO BETTELHEIM,
THE USES OF ENCHANTMENT

ON MY SIXTH BIRTHDAY, I was given a little green mop
and bucket, enchantingly kid-scaled. Also a baby doll. The
mop held my attention. It was fun to swish the twisted strands
around the floor, nominally making it cleaner, and I got the
point of the job: it started, it ended, you felt proud. The doll
mystified me. The limbs were rigid; the eyes glared. I couldn't
make it go on adventures in my mind like I could my collection of stuffed animals—fearless rabbit, leopard seal, koala.

Nor did it squish under my arm in a companionable manner while I went about my business.

I viewed this doll with suspicion, as an inducement to take up some dubious enthusiasm that was going to turn out, Tom Sawyer–like, to be work in the way the mop and bucket were not. This was not an age when people wallowed in parenting. Kids like my parents got married and started having children right away, before they even knew what they were giving up to do it. My mother was everywhere and nowhere, constant but peripheral, the separate acts of care like salt grains dissolved in water. It was hard to see where the fun of it was.

The psychoanalyst Adam Phillips writes that the mother "hates the infant for the child's ruthless use of her." My mother's body was indistinguishable from mine—to me, at least. I owned it. I poked at the constellation of freckles on her arm while sitting bored in a church pew; I dragged on her hand, swinging, when she walked down the grocery aisles, my brother the counterweight on her other hand. "Stop *hanging* on me," she would say, fretfully, despairingly. We would gape, shocked that she didn't consider us all a single being, like a grove of aspens is said to be. Then we would resume our tugging.

The bedtime song she sang to us most nights was "Babes in the Woods," in which two children are stolen and then lost in the forest. We clamored for its lilting melody: "They sobbed and they sighed, and they bitterly cried, / and the poor little children, they laid down and died." Here we tucked ourselves side by side under her arm to savor their fate. "And when they were dead, the robins so red, / took strawberry leaves and over them spread."

Her mother no doubt sang it to her, and had been sung it herself. My grandmother was the ninth child in an immigrant German farm family, the kind whose idea of a fun game was throwing live chickens at each other. In my imagination they hadn't read but rather lived Grimm, those unsentimental tales with swift, implacable revenges, with rifts between parents and children taken for granted. The song fit us, even if I didn't consciously grasp that sometimes my mother might have wanted to lose us, too.

My brother, Christian, was a benevolent dictator, though only eleven months older than I; Irish twins, they call it. Early on we got the idea that it would be sensible to look after each other, and our private mythology of brother and sister as the two faces of a coin, around which so much of our lives has taken shape, was forged before we could both speak. I recently found a snapshot of the two of us hand in hand, walking ourselves to kindergarten. It's taken from behind and we don't know we're being watched. Our white knee socks are pulled very high. Who took it—my mother or my father? What were they thinking as we set off on our own?

Those wild strawberries: they were a thrilling signpost of danger for anyone alert to the presence of magic in the world. "Brother, come and dance with me," coaxes Gretel in the opera by Engelbert Humperdinck (true name!) that we checked out from the local library. She and Hansel break the milk pitcher and spill their poor supper, and their furious mother sends them into the woods to gather strawberries as twilight gathers. You know the rest. The witch is immolated, the mother repents; the child psychologist Bruno Bettelheim suggested that they are, to the child, the same person, and that "the child can become himself only as the parent is defeated."

Soon enough we children were looking after children ourselves. Press-ganged by neighbor parents, I noted their eagerness to leave, how they rattled off emergency numbers while the car keys jingled. We were terrible babysitters, impatient, insincere. The kids knew it. One used to ask accusingly, every single day after school, "What are *you* doing here, stupid?" I gave up babysitting as soon as I got a work permit and could clear plates for two dollars an hour plus tips.

Around this time, in the back room of a record store I found a 1920s movie poster of two plump children asleep under a blanket of curled brown leaves. *Babes in the Woods*, said the poster: *A Gorgeous Tale of Charm and Adventure for Young and Old.* That was an optimistic way to characterize the plotline. Did the kids die in the Hollywood version, eulogized by robins? I tacked it to my bedroom wall. At sixteen I was already nostalgic for our childhood, for the time when the two of us were alone together by choice and not by social fiat, even though my brother was just there on the other side of the wall, besieged. I was doing nothing to help.

From birth, Christian had an innate sense of flair and ceremony: in elementary school, indifferent to mockery, he would cut our peanut butter and jelly into crustless tea sandwiches and include a fluted paper plate in our lunch bags. By adolescence, this aesthetic sensitivity had toughened into a defiant flamboyance, which took breathtaking moral—and sometimes physical—courage to carry off in 1983 New England. The high school cafeteria was a site of martyrdom. Injustices done to him—Brad Crawley throwing Suzy Qs at my beautiful and rare brother!—made my skin burn with caustic fury. But I didn't have any great plan for saving him. I was dealing with issues of misfitness, too, though instead of blazing, as he did, I moped and skulked. He left for college and the house was horribly quiet. No one to dance around waving a dish towel and singing *Sweeney Todd* while I did the dishes.

But as the story happens, we went off to school together again, the first of many thousand-mile drives in a 1974 Chevy Impala with a Styrofoam cooler of fried chicken in the backseat. I'd only bothered to apply to one college. Had he decided ahead of time, in his imperious way, that I'd follow him to his? It was an excellent school for the sprawl of things I was interested in, but that seemed almost a lucky coincidence. It was unimaginable that we would be separated, though I regretted that he'd picked a punishing climate. Lake Michigan froze in chaotic slabs all the way out to the horizon.

At college, I was delighted and relieved to find that he was loved. Potheads, sorority girls, supercilious professors, and ROTC cadets adored him for his absurdist wit and his air of having trailed a little bit of splendor behind him, like the bright winter smell that follows you in from outside.

Christian presented me to all his various social groups with an almost belligerent confidence that I would be taken in, too. He taught me how to pull a respectable bong hit, how to find the nerve to fling myself into a pool of conversation, and how to sign up for the right classes—that is to say, those with the least practical application: Introduction to the Art Song, the Seven Hills of Augustan Rome, a seminar on semiotic inside jokes in *The Name of the Rose*. "Come on, sister, have yourself a ball!" the Kinks song went; I heard it for the first time on a body-swallowing sofa while getting high with his new friends. "Don't be afraid to come dancing, / it's only natural."

That first year I was away, one of my small band of outsider friends back home got pregnant. We'd all been strenuously taught that being a teen mother meant the death of hope, but she was doing cooler things than any of us had or would, and she made college look like a desperately bourgeois choice. She had a record contract, she toured, and now she played her electric guitar slung sidesaddle to her enormous belly. I thought that she, if anyone, might be able to invent a new kind of motherhood. But when I visited, the baby cried and cried and cried and cried, creating a sort of huge ear-popping pressure that shoved all thought out of the room. I quietly got up to leave—it somehow seemed almost an indecent thing to witness. My indomitable friend stood with her back to me, gripping the porcelain of the kitchen sink, and said dully, "Please don't go." Even her bright mind seemed ground down. Her bravery terrified me, and so did the foreverness of what she'd done.

I still feel the ecstatic release of driving away from that house along the coast road, the long way around just because I could, twiddling the radio dial for a good midnight song to rinse away the static. And for a long while, that is all I thought about the subject of babies, other than trying not to have one accidentally. Every now and then I'd squint my eyes to visualize a time when I'd start feeling the craving myself: when I was thirty, it would be at thirty-two; at thirty-two, I'd be ready by thirty-six; and on it went. I was hitching a ride on Zeno's arrow, speeding toward a target I'd never reach. Boyfriends were only too grateful, I imagined, not to have the "Where is this relationship going?" conversation.

A job as a book editor took me to London, where Christian had gone to work as a theatrical agent, and after a gap of a decade we once more lived close by. If I felt lonely, I could put a coat on over my nightgown and walk unnoticed through the sleazy all-night carnival of Old Compton Street to hang out at the flat he shared with Mikey, his boyfriend and then, once England discreetly began to allow civil unions, his legal partner. Christian and I spent our professional lives looking after people in sometimes fragile emotional circumstances. It is not easy being a creative person, and oftentimes the tantrums that were thrown, the vulnerabilities that cracked open and needed to be patched up again, could be wearying and unnerving to cope with. Like looking after children, but without the adorability to seduce you into not minding so much. "The world," he said to me darkly one of those evenings, "has enough people. You and I do not need to add to them." And I was happy to sign this latest treaty of mutual support and defense.

Scientists say that our pupils flare when they register something of interest; for women, babies top the list. (Porn follows.) But my pupils and my hypothalamus, the seat of desire, did not seem to be communicating. There was no corresponding baby hunger, at least not in that ready place where all my other hungers were shouting for attention. Meanwhile, there had been a societal swing back to the orthodoxy of motherhood. Serious journalists wrote with anguish of their biological clocks, a term I came to hate. Twins in strollers wide as combines mowed the sidewalks, the result of untold numbers of women over thirty-seven enduring a hypodermic in the behind. All of a sudden it was de rigueur for rising stars to be photographed lusciously, peachily pregnant. But a dwindling number of my babyless friends admitted, very quietly indeed, that they weren't so sure they wanted one, not just now but ever—like a group of medieval heretics muttering agnosticism at a time when that could get you a date with a stake and some matches.

All the available cultural artifacts seemed to be telling us holdouts that if you were a woman, your business was having a baby, and if you didn't, there was something wrong—with your body, meaning you couldn't conceive, or your mind, meaning you couldn't conceive of it. So perhaps this absence of desire in me really was pathological. Dutifully, I added it to the list of things to talk over with my therapist. I could chitchat with her for costly hours about my complicated feelings on this and that—but not, I found, on this subject. I studied the inoffensive museum prints on the wall of her little room, watching her hands lying folded and waiting in her lap. We both, I think, wished I had something more to say.

I wondered often what she hoped I would do. I sensed she wanted me to be courageous, to be bigger than just myself. But she, impeccable Freudian, kept her counsel. Not so others. Is there any other situation in life where people feel so free to tell you what to do, short of checking you in to rehab? "I'd get on with it, if you're going to do it," said the gynecologist, blunt as a speculum. "And sooner rather than later." I didn't recall having asked her opinion. A literary agent who'd had enough kids to populate a string quartet told me over lunch that I would regret my decision, but by then it would be too late, and she smacked her hand down on the table so our water glasses sloshed. (What decision? What and when had I decided?) Another woman held both my hands, her eyes drilling into mine, and said that for her, having children was like flicking on the light in a dark room. *But the older I get,* I thought mutinously to myself, *the more I like a bit of dim lighting. At forty, it's easier on the complexion.*

In the meantime, Christian and I had taken to pointing to each other.

You do it.

No, *you* do it.

And we laughed.

———

So much of being a grown-up is about managing or quelling desires. For food, for drink, for sex, for good times; if you're a woman, I maintain, for ambition. You should not want *too* much. It is strange, then, to be in a position where society demands you should have an appetite for something. And yet here was a rare instance where I was appetite-free, and the world seemed to be saying, "You have to want this thing, if only so that we can help you work through your feelings about not having it!"

And so I set about trying to try, with the same enthusiasm that I would have brought to cooking a Thanksgiving dinner and sitting down joylessly to chew the whole thing myself.

Here's where I tell you that I love children, and where you look at me skeptically. But I do. I love them for their wild experiments with language; for their inability to feign interest in things that do not truly grip them; for their seriousness and total immersion in play.

But when you talk of not wanting children, it is impossible to avoid sounding defensive, like you're trying to prove the questionable beauty of a selfish and too-tidy existence. It is hard to come across as anything other than brittle, rigid, controlling, against life itself. Anyway, I resented having to explain myself at all, to open a hatch over my heart because a near stranger asked an impertinent question.

A writer friend, defending her choice not to, said, "Boredom in children is useful. Boredom in adults is not." I, too, was sometimes aghast at the short-fibered thoughts of my friends whose small children beseeched or bellowed as their stories were begun again and again and never finished, whereas I got to spoil myself with long hours of unspooling daydreams. (A nagging thought: What did I have to show for all that free time the mothers didn't have?) But it's also true that I was staggered by the transformation of these women. Their devotion, their patience (not something I'd always noted in them before the kids came). They were not showing off; this was not display. There was no statute saying they had to give themselves over so completely. They were going to wipe the face, wipe the bottom, feed, bathe, lull, teach by word, teach by example, read the books, put away the toys, buy the tiny clothes, six months later buy a slightly larger set of clothes, fret about the schools, and on and on; the caring and the worry was never, ever, ever going to stop, not until death. I wasn't sure I had it in me. Perhaps I was a kind of human geode: sparkly and hollow.

Still, I did give it a go. Never let it be said that I wasn't willing to get on a scary amusement park ride at least once, even if I bent the safety bar with my grip. But the big joke after all that brinksmanship in my twenties—tense days of waiting for a period to show up after some delicious act of heedlessness—was that it isn't so easy to get pregnant. And I didn't. I wasn't relieved, but I wasn't sorry either. I felt with some satisfaction that my body had honorably answered for my whole family this lingering question of whether there would be a next generation of Hodells. I'd done my duty, and now we could all move on.

The two kids with their high white socks were now undeniably middle-aged. One afternoon, Christian e-mailed to say that he and Mikey had something important they wanted to talk to me about. His Important Conversations could be unpredictable and sometimes terrifying: Why He Is the Wrong Boyfriend for You; Your Job Is a Poisoned Chalice; That Lipstick Shade Does Not Flatter. (We all feared the familiar words "I'm going to say this with love . . .") We skyped; I trained my face to look serenely receptive.

But this time, it was not about me. The comedy of it! While my family had glanced covertly my way, wondering when I'd get around to marrying, my gay brother had gone and done it. And now, while they'd politely held their tongues on the subject of grandkids, he'd visited a clinic in Connecticut to flip through binders full of baby mamas. He and Mikey squeezed close so they'd both fit onto my monitor to tell me that they'd picked an egg donor with a profile that suited, and with luck and a hundred thousand dollars, in a year's time they'd be parents. I hadn't even known they were considering it. Yet it made total sense to me that Mikey wanted children. An atmosphere of calm hangs about him like a cloud cap on a green mountain. Everyone in need of balm seeks him out: the anxious and the shy, little kids, old people. He's one of the secret, mighty soothers and nurturers of this world.

It's not that Christian has nothing of this in him. Once I'd passed a shop window and stopped dead at a little bronze meerkat up on its hind legs, scouting trouble in wait for its troupe. I bought it at once: it looked exactly like him. But our pact! What he'd said about the too many other people! I forgot that I'd been at least a little ready to break the pact, too.

They found a surrogate, the magnificent and sainted Sharla, who lived all the way out in Wichita, Kansas. The Connecticut clinic frothed with activity. Both Mikey and Christian contributed—I didn't ask, but I imagined it involved specialized magazines in a toilet stall—and this was eyedroppered onto the eggs vacuumed up that same day from the donor they'd met for a few nervous minutes before she was wheeled in for the procedure, and whom they had forgotten to get a photo with for posterity. "We've got fifteen embryos in the freezer," Christian reported expansively. "You could have one of Mikey's, if you want."

Sharla was flown to the clinic, and two embryos—one of each flavor—were implanted. I was visiting Christian in London when he got the news of a strong single heartbeat, sitting in his fishbowl office with all his employees clapping and cheering around him. He rejoiced with them, and we all cracked each others' spines with hugs like a convention of chiropractors, but when he shut the door, tears glazed his eyes. "I mind that there aren't two."

Soon, Sharla e-mailed ultrasounds in which a little bean could be seen and then not seen, inky and blurred like an old mezzotint. Christian and Mikey talked baby names for hours. "Now let's do jewels! Ruby. Pearl? *Jade*." Soon it was Lusitania, Waterloo, Wichita.

In the end, she was Elsa. I flew to Kansas on her birth to be housekeeper while they figured out how to be parents. Christian was Papa; Mikey was Daddy. But the dot of blood harvested when she was minutes old would show that she was Christian's biological child. That's *mine*, he whispered disbelievingly. It would take a month to get Elsa's documents in order, and they rented a paper-walled suite in a sort of shantytown for transient executives. Sharla pumped as much breast milk as she could muster. Bottles of it sat, unsettlingly yellow, in the fridge among our groceries. This generous stranger, no blood of ours, had the most sustained physical relation to Elsa of any of us. She had made her—or rather, she'd allowed Elsa to make herself inside her, spinning her little body from the genetic material of my brother and a pretty, brown-eyed law student of Hungarian extraction from Rhode Island whom none of us would ever see again.

Not everyone falls in love with a newborn. That is this auntie's secret. Elsa was a red and wrinkly visitor from outer space, skinny, with a slightly lopsided face and opaque, mineral-blue eyes that minutely raked the face of whoever was bent over her with the bottle, searching as her little mouth worked. Things were most definitely going on in there, but who could say what? Her squalls were spasmodic, weak, shuddering, as if her small bones weren't sturdy enough to withstand the gusts of wanting. Christian found her crying somehow hilarious. When I welled up at the noises of grief, he snapped, "Are you drunk?" He snatched up Elsa, who was swaddled like a canapé, and speed skated around the living room in his socks, singing Christmas carols. Elsa stared up at him transfixed, plastered into the crook of his arm. He whisked past me. "There's Tatie Courtney!"

This was the shocker. He was a natural father: easy, confident, fearless. How was he allowed to be different from me?

Wichita seemed to be all mall, and we toured them in the enormous rented SUV, shopping for the numerous bulky items necessary for the comfort of a week-old baby. Christian was explaining how her life was going to go. "She'll ski, she'll speak French, and she'll play tennis and the piano. Everything else she gets to pick for herself."

The atmosphere in the car shifted a little; I could tell he was working up to something. I glanced over at his profile with the ribbon of Kansas beyond it. His Byronic swoop of hair was clipped like Caesar's now, but he'd grown into his handsome nose, and I thought he looked very distinguished and not at all improbable at the wheel of the big car.

"Tell me about the . . . about the coochie." He couldn't quite get the word out.

"You mean the vagina?" I bit down a laugh. Really I was thrilled to be asked about a subject I could at last feel learned about. "First of all, think of it as a kind of self-cleaning oven. You don't need to get up in there with any soap or whatnot. It takes care of itself as long as you keep the outside area clean, and . . ." So I went on.

His knuckles tightened on the steering wheel after a time.

"Okay, that's great. I don't think I can hear any more right now." He appeared to be breathing through his mouth. "But thanks. Really helpful."

Poor boy. I realized I didn't know if he'd ever seen a vagina up close, and now he was in charge of making someone feel okay about hers. We steered into a consoling Krispy Kreme drive-through with the "Hot Now" sign lit up. I had the feeling that the next time he'd ask me for advice would be in a decade, when the dreaded menses loomed.

Elsa was no longer than my forearm, and there was just so much turbulence ahead. Girls are born with all the eggs they will ever have, enough to populate a small city. But these start dying off at birth, and only a few hundred of them will kick off into the fallopian tubes and mature into the big chance. Women have, I would guess, about two decades of genuine, galloping fertility. With twelve periods a year, that's 240 shots at making a baby without enlisting a team of professionals and some lottery winnings. Why was I thinking about this already? She was a few weeks old. This was the telescoping nature of human endeavor. All the flailing around, the mad activity—going to parties, falling in love, buying houses, striving at work—could be smashed like a soda can into this flat fact: we have children so they can have children so they can have children. I had a blast of vertigo, as when you look into a puddle and see the stars falling away behind your head.

Elsa got her passport, Sharla's milk dried up, and we all dispersed, exhausted: Mikey and Christian to a wholly altered life, with unrecognizable hours and fears and blisses, and me back to mine, where there was still a sock lying in the middle of the rug and an empty glass in the sink.

I'm no Facebooker, but I started checking in daily to see photos of them settling in, 3,500 miles away. One morning, Christian posted: *Last day of my paternity leave. Devastated. My little angel is five weeks old today. From this moment on, everything I do is for her and her wonderful daddy.*

Here it was: I'd been kicked out of our tiny Narnia. The wardrobe held only coats. The cold stone in my chest was the rightness of what he'd written. In his novel *On the Black Hill*, Bruce Chatwin describes grown twins: "Because they knew each other's thoughts, they even quarreled without speaking." Now my brother was thinking and feeling things I never would. In college he'd taught me how to speak, but this was something I could never say aloud: *Don't leave me behind.*

The only recourse was to love this little scrap of a human, and in the first really adult way I would love anyone. Without expectations of returned affection. Without wounded vanity. With foreknowledge of impending boredom, of exasperation, of anger that I could not allow myself to nurse. In the understanding that I would sometimes be ridiculous in her eyes. Knowing I did not have the rights of parenthood, I could make no demands of her beyond those any grown-up would make of a child: *Hold my hand; we're crossing the street.*

———

The ruthlessness I feared, the ruthlessness I knew in myself as a child, turns out not to be the point of the tale. There are times when the parent enjoys being feasted upon.

When Nathan, my boyfriend of five years, held Elsa for the first time, he wept—big sparklers caught in his lower eyelashes, too light to drop. "Not sadness," he said, "just big feeling." Now the decision is made. But the decision is not past. No matter how it came about—was it my procrastination; disinclination; anxiety; self-absorption?—we live with its consequences every day. Nathan is younger than I am, and it's a little odd to be dealing at his age with the question of whether he will have his own children or not. For as long as he chooses to be here with me, it will be the latter. I want him to stay, but it is, as they say, a big ask.

I've learned from the work of the primatologist Sarah Hrdy that aunts exist in nature. Of course they are everywhere, biologically speaking, but some (marmosets and langurs, I'm looking at you) truly behave as the aunt I want to be, the aunt I have already become, and this is called allomothering. They will feed, groom, hold, and carry a child when they have had none of their own. So there is a word for what this is that I'm doing, I and all my sisters of the genetic dead end. Whatever I've learned in this life will not stop with me; I'll teach it to Elsa.

From feeling we move to thinking, and then to doing. "If there is a kindness instinct," writes Adam Phillips, "it is going to have to take onboard ambivalence in human relations. It is kind to be able to bear conflict, in oneself and others; it is kind, to oneself and others, to forgo magic and sentimentality for reality." As night falls in the forest, Hansel crowns Gretel Queen of the Woods and sings to her, "I give you the strawberries, but don't eat them all." It is hard, so hard, to let go of a story you've lived by. Brother, good-bye; father, hello. As in the fairy tales, there must be a gift at a christening, and this one is my offering: for her, the wild strawberries will only be strawberries, and sweet. "*Fraises des bois*, Elsa darling," my brother will say. "Try one."

MATERNAL INSTINCTS

by

Laura Kipnis

"LIKE SHITTING A PUMPKIN" is how radical feminist Shulamith Firestone famously described childbirth, though she hadn't had the experience herself; it was a friend's report on what labor was like, shortly after the happy event. It only confirmed Firestone's view that childbearing was barbaric, and pregnancy should be abolished. Beyond the personal discomfort, her larger point was that women aren't going to achieve social equality until some technological alternative is invented to save us from being the only sex expected to go through it. If men were the ones forced to endure this ordeal, obviously such a technological solution would long ago have been devised.

Firestone was clearly no fan of Nature, an animus I find myself reliving whenever I hear people, especially women, espousing such supposedly "natural" facts as maternal instinct and mother-child bonds. It's not that I think these things don't exist; they certainly do. They exist as social conventions of womanhood at this moment in history, not as eternal conditions, because what's social is also malleable.

But what's with all the sentimentality about nature anyway, and the kowtowing to it, as though adhering to the "natural" had some sort of ethical force? It's not like nature is such a *friend* to womankind, not like nature doesn't just blithely kill women off on a random basis during childbirth or anything. No one who faces up to the real harshness of nature can feel very benignly about its tyranny. Sure, we like nature when it's a beautiful day on the beach; less so when a tidal wave kills your family or a shark bites off your arm. If it were up to nature, women would devote themselves to propagating the species, compliantly serving as life's passive instruments, and pipe down on the social demands. It's only modern technology's role in *overriding* nature—lowering the maternal death rate, inventing decent birth control methods—that's offered women some modicum of self-determination. If it comes down to a choice, my vote's with technology and modernity, which have liberated women far more than getting the vote or any other feminist initiative (important as these have been), precisely by rescuing us from nature's clutches.

But my quarrel with the concept of maternal instinct isn't why I never had kids myself. I was never particularly opposed to the idea of having kids—let no one say that I don't love kids! It always seemed like an interesting future possibility, the same way that joining the Peace Corps someday seemed like an interesting future possibility. And though neither possibility ever consolidated into action, I still feel I've done my share when it comes to ensuring the future of humanity. Let no one say that I didn't spend the equivalent of a year's college tuition hauling my beloved niece and two nephews to the movies regularly during their formative years, bribing them into good behavior with pricey buckets of popcorn and gallons of soda. Let no one say that I didn't do my best to imbue them with my values (social rebellion, critical thinking), and subtly shape them in my image, a project that continues to this day—at holidays I like to slip them hundred-dollar bills with my picture taped over Franklin's. "Who's your favorite grown-up?" I wheedle, when their parents are out of earshot. Under my careful tutelage, they've evolved into fast-talking and ironically hilarious little wiseasses, tolerating and mocking my improvement campaigns; pocketing the cash; pretending to note my reading suggestions and life lessons. I think we understand one another.

No, despite my proven talents at nurturing, I don't believe in maternal instinct because as anyone who's perused the literature on the subject knows, it's an invented concept that arises at a particular point in history (I'm speaking of Western history here)—circa the Industrial Revolution, just as the new industrial-era sexual division of labor was being negotiated, the one where men go to work and women stay home raising kids. (Before that, pretty much everyone worked at home.) The new line was that such arrangements were handed down by nature. As family historians tell us, this is also when the romance of the child begins—ironically it was only when children's actual economic value declined, because they were no longer necessary additions to the household labor force, that they became the priceless little treasures we know them as today. Once they started costing more to raise than they contributed to the household economy, there had to be *some* justification for having them, which is when the story that having children was a big emotionally fulfilling thing first started taking hold.

It also took a decline in infant-mortality rates for mothers to start regarding their offspring with much affection. When infant deaths were high (in England before 1800 mortality rates were 15 to 30 percent in the first year of life), maternal attachment ran understandably low. As historian Lawrence Stone pointed out, giving a newborn child the same name as a dead sibling was a common practice; in other words, children were barely regarded as distinct individuals. They were also typically sent to wet nurses following birth—so much for the mother-child bond—and when economic circumstances were dire, farmed out to foundling hospitals or workhouses ("little more than licensed death camps," said Stone). But then childhood as such really didn't exist, or at least it wasn't a recognizable concept, as historian Philippe Ariès documented; this, too, is a social invention. Children were viewed as small adults; apprenticed out to work at age five. It was only as families began getting smaller—birthrates declined steeply in the nineteenth century—that the emotional value of each child increased. Which is where we find the origin point for most of our current ideas about maternal fulfillment.

All I'm saying is that what we're calling biological instinct is a historical artifact—a culturally specific development, not a fact of nature. An invented instinct can feel entirely real (I'm sure it can feel profound), though before we get too sentimental, let's not forget that human maternity has also had a fairly checkered history over the ages, including such maternal traditions as infanticide, child abandonment, cruelty, and abuse.

But the real reason I'm against the romance about maternal instincts is that what gets lost amid this fealty to nature is that nature hasn't been particularly kind to women, and I say we owe it no favors in return. If women have been "ensnared by nature" as Simone de Beauvoir (no fan of maternity herself) put it, if it's so far been our biological situation that we're the ones stuck bearing the children, then there should be a lot more social recompense and reparations for this inequity than there are. The reason these have been slow in coming? Because women keep forgetting to demand them, so convinced are we that these social arrangements are the "natural" order of things. The willingness to call an inequitable situation "natural" puts us on the royal path to being society's chumps.

Even though I never actually ruled out having kids, I

suppose I wasn't that deeply identified with the prospect of maternity either, which meant that I was always a little more casual about birth control than a fully cognizant anatomical female probably should be. I never entirely connected sex and procreation—it didn't help that I generally used methods you don't have to actively think about, like IUDs—which resulted in a few pregnancies over the years whenever I took a month or two off between the previous model and its successor. Pregnancies are useful for clarifying one's life priorities, of course, but they also clarify a lot about the prevailing conditions of motherhood when you're deciding whether or not to sign on for the long haul.

The second to last time I got pregnant, I was in a long-term relationship, which is one of the usual practical considerations for those contemplating motherhood. My boyfriend and I had been living together for about five years at that point—we'd stay together for twelve and eventually even buy a house together—meaning we were stable enough, and financially comfortable enough. Except that he was the bass player in a well-known jazz band and thus on the road about half the year, and I'd just received a three-year fellowship at the University of Michigan and was planning to commute by train between Ann Arbor and Chicago when my boyfriend was in town (though he promised to come up for weekends when he could). Contemplating the result of the pregnancy test, I envisioned myself on the train lugging a baby, a computer (they were a lot heavier in those days), books, and the requisite ton of baby paraphernalia, and I couldn't imagine how I'd carry all that stuff. I thought about giving up the fellowship (for about a nanosecond), but this didn't seem like the wisest life choice, as I'd been lucky beyond belief to get it. My boyfriend, too, had his dream gig—he wasn't about to give it up (and even if he had, then do what for money, play bar mitzvahs?). It took me about ten seconds—far less time than it took to type this paragraph—to conclude that having a baby was unfeasible, or not feasible under the current conditions of isolate do-the-best-you-can parenthood. I had an abortion.

I realize, looking back, that the image of myself struggling on the train with too much baggage was analogous to my sense of what being a mother would feel like: weighted down and immobilized, though my ambivalence surely had as much to do with my perception of the social role of "mother" as with diaper bags. (I probably could have bought a car for the commute instead of struggling on the train—I later did just that.) But one of the pleasures of living with a jazz musician was picking up and meeting him in far-flung places on short notice, or traveling as a band girlfriend for stretches: jaunts to Japan, Europe, Omaha. I learned to pack light and not carp about delays. (Also to go through a different customs line than the band unless I wanted every last toiletry opened and sniffed.) I liked having the kind of life where you didn't know what was going to come next; the opposite of what life as a mother would be, or so I presumed.

Some might adduce that my getting pregnant (yes, more than once) suggests that I was more eager to embark on the path of motherhood than I'm letting on. Maybe so, but I think not—it's not like I agonized about having abortions or regretted them later. I was willing to contemplate kids, though if I'm being honest, among the factors militating against it was my profound dread of being conscripted into the community of other mothers—the sociality of the playground and day-care center, and at the endless activities and lessons that are de rigueur in today's codes of upper-middle-class parenting. It terrified me. For one thing, I've never been good at small talk, or female conventionality. Also, the mothers I met struck me as a strange and unenviable breed: harried, hampered, resentful. I didn't want to accidentally become one of them. I know there are unparalleled joys in having children—the deep love for another creature; the connection to a greater human purpose. But then there are the day-to-day realities. Let's face it: children's intellectual capacities and conversational acumen are not their best features. Boredom and intellectual atrophy are the normal conditions of daily life for the child-raising classes. All of which I could see all too plainly on the faces of the other women around the swing set when I hauled my beloved niece and nephews to various playgrounds or trotted them around to kiddie museums over the years. Not to mention (how to put this politely?) that child raising is not what you'd call a socially valued activity in our time despite the endless sanctimony about how important it is, which those doing the labor of it can't help being furious about—quietly furious about being dropped down a few dozen rungs in the social-equity ranks. You have to wonder:

Is it really such a great idea to rely on the more aggrieved sex—those whose emotional needs are most socially disparaged, whose labors are most undervalued, and who may consequently be a little . . . on edge—to do the vast majority of the child rearing?

Lately I've been hearing from childless female friends and acquaintances about their sense of being judged by this community of other women for not having children, as though their *not* having children betrays all the women who took a hit for the team. I can't say I ever felt any such disapproval myself (maybe I was just oblivious), or family pressure, but apparently it can be intense. (I recently said to my mother, "How come you never pressured me to have kids?" She rolled her eyes and said, "What good would it have done?") But then you also hear from friends and acquaintances who *have* had kids about feeling judged by the community of other mothers for such things as not pureeing their own organic baby food, or other failures to comply with the many heightened requirements set by today's former careerists turned full-time moms.

Apparently, the more "progressive" the community, the more intense the inducements to do it all "naturally"—once again, nature and women locked in some sort of master-slave dialectic. I listen, I ponder, and in my darkest heart, I think that motherhood today is no less deforming than when Betty Friedan detailed maternal malaise in 1960; it just takes updated forms. Women are still angry about feeling duped and undervalued, but instead of ignoring their kids and downing cocktails all day, as in Friedan's time, now we have the angry overdrive child-rearing style: motherhood as a competitive sport.

Back to women and nature. Let me say something possibly controversial in the hopes of clarifying something else. When it comes to female anatomy, it's not only being saddled with the entire excruciating, immobilizing burden (sorry, "privilege") of childbearing that we're dealing with (a privilege that can kill you, thanks). It gets worse. Among nature's other little jokes at women's expense is the placement of the clitoris, a primary locale of female sexual pleasure, at some remove from the vagina, a primary locale of human sexual intercourse. Perhaps this mainly affects women who have sex with men, but that's still a majority of us, because apparently some percentage of men don't automatically fathom these anatomical complexities, or so say researchers who collect data on women's orgasm rates compared to men's. On this score, women lag far behind. (I realize that orgasms aren't the sole index of sexual pleasure, but surely they're *something*.)

Now, we could account for the orgasm gap between men and women by simply concluding that women are anatomically constructed in such a way that a certain amount of sexual dissatisfaction comes with the territory, and leave it at that. But mostly we don't say that, because even though the anatomy in question can be enlisted to tell that story, it's not the socially favored narrative at the moment. The preferred story is that women and men are entitled to sexual equity; sexual pleasure is as much a woman's right as a man's—even the men's magazines say so! In fact, it's now such a mainstream view that network sitcoms make jokes about it. Pretty much everyone these days knows that with a small amount of reeducation and patient communication, men can be schooled into becoming better lovers. A lot of men these days even take pride in developing such skills—I've seen T-shirts to this effect.

My point is that women have been a lot more inventive at demanding sexual pleasure than at demanding maternity reform. When it comes to sexual pleasure, whatever inequities nature has imposed on women can be overcome: in other words, culture overrides anatomy. Yet when it comes to maternity, somehow everyone's a raging biological determinist. Not only are women fated to be the designated child *bearers* in this story, but this mostly still translates into their taking on the social role of raising them, too. Even with men doing more parenting than before, the majority of women are still left facing the well-rehearsed motherhood-versus-career dichotomy. But it's *not* a dichotomy; it's a socially organized choice masquerading as a natural one. There would be all sorts of ways to organize society and sexuality that don't create false choices if we simply got inventive about it—as inventive as we've been about equity in sexual pleasure—but there has to be the political will to do it. There has to be the right story going in.

It must be said that women themselves haven't helped much here, at least not those who go around touting our mystical relation to nature—maternal instincts, mother-child bonds, and so on. According to Diane Eyer's *Mother-Infant Bonding*, the concept that bonding has any biological basis is "scientific fictionalizing." Bonding research has been dismissed by most of the scientific community as an ideological rather than a scientific premise, Eyer says, driven by popular concepts about natural womanhood and a woman's place being in the home. No one ever talked about such bonds before the rise of industrialization, when wage labor first became an option for women. Note that the bonding story got revved up again in the early 1970s, as women were moving into the labor market (screwing up traditional conceptions about the natural female role), popularized by child development experts like pediatrician T. Berry Brazelton, who said that mothers who don't stay at home bonding with their children for the first year spawn delinquents and terrorists.

So the question we're left with is this: What's the most advantageous story to adopt about female biology and nature? If we keep telling the one about nature speaking to women in a direct hookup from womb to brain, then guess what? This *will* parlay into who should do the social job of child rearing and under what conditions. Men will have less reason to sign up for child-rearing equity (assuming there's a man in the picture), day care will *never* be a social entitlement like public education, and the issue of how to manage a child and a job will continue to remain each lone woman's individual dilemma to solve, even when that job is an economic necessity, as is certainly the case for the majority of mothers today.

———

At one point, in my late thirties, I thought for a bit about having a child on my own. I was no longer with the musician boyfriend. My next boyfriend and I occasionally fantasized about having a kid—he even once proposed during such a reverie, on a romantic boat trip—but though we were together for years, we couldn't get along for a sufficient stretch of time to accomplish either marrying or procreating. After we split up, I wasn't in anything very serious with anyone for a while, though there was a man I used to roll around with on a casual basis. When I told him I was thinking about having a kid, he said he'd be happy to try to get me pregnant if I wanted, though he didn't want to be involved in raising a child. So that was one practicality taken care of, at least. I approached my sister, the one who'd borne my beloved niece and nephews, to ask whether, if I had a kid, it could sort of lodge with her while I was at work or out of town—she had so many kids underfoot already, one more wouldn't be that noticeable. I'm sorry to say that she laughed in my face (though in a kindly way, she instructs me to add). When she got done laughing, she explained that it was a well-known fact that no nanny or babysitter would work in a house with four children; three was the limit. I tried guilt-tripping her, but she wasn't biting. The single motherhood idea faded away a short time later.

When I hear pundits going on lately about the declining birthrate and the graying of the population, I know that it's all my fault. In case you haven't heard, birthrates across the industrialized world have been in steep decline ever since the advent of the Pill. (While an overpopulation crisis looms in the developing world, underpopulation hits this part of the globe.) Though it wasn't due to the Pill alone: once women started entering institutes of higher education in increasing numbers, and the job market opened its arms (if not its coffers), birthrates plummeted even further. As much as women talk the talk about maternal instinct, fewer than ever are walking the walk: the fastest-growing segments of the female population now have either zero children or one child by age forty. According to demographers, the consequences down the road will be seismic: an aging citizenry unable to sustain itself economically (Social Security is already basically a national Ponzi scheme, some are calculating).

Though no one exactly says it, women are voting with their ovaries, and the reason is simple. There are too few social supports, especially given the fact that the majority of women are no longer just mothers now, they're mother-workers. Yet virtually no social policy accounts for this. Interestingly, women with the most education are the ones having the fewest children, though even basic literacy has a negative effect on birthrates in the developing world—the higher the literacy rate, the lower the birthrate. In other words, when women acquire critical skills and start weighing their options, they soon wise up to the fact that they're not getting enough recompense for their labors. In trade union terms, you'd call it a production slowdown, though in places like Japan the birthrate has fallen so drastically it's more of a full-fledged strike. Over there it's prompting national soul-searching, appointed commissions, and even some discussion of a previously unheard-of option: more social welfare spending on mothers and children.

And what about here? Maintaining the species is something the United States, too, would appear to have a stake in. But until there's a better social deal for women—not just fathers doing more child care but vastly more social resources directed at the situation, including teams of well-paid professionals on standby (*not* low-wage-earning women with their own children at home)—birthrates will certainly continue to plummet.

In retrospect, not having children feels to me like having dodged a bullet. I think the lifestyle would have felt too constraining, too routine, though I do sometimes encounter women who seem to manage it with panache. (Usually these are women with the resources for lots of child care.) Still, I confess to feeling an unseemly little pleasure at having eluded nature's snare, saying "fuck you" to all that, though nature's going to get us all in the end, obviously. It's also my little "fuck you" to a society that sentimentalizes children except when it comes to allocating enough resources to raising them, and that would include elevating the 22 percent of children currently living in poverty to a decent standard of living.

If "maternal instinct" is a synonym for wanting to devote your life to something, or be absorbed in someone other than yourself, then fine. But its having been invented in the first place means there's no reason such an instinct can't be invented differently, including in men. Men may not yet be able to biologically bear children (though how far off can that day be, or Firestone's dream of test tube offspring?), but when women no longer have an exclusive relation to such things, no doubt raising children will become a more socially valued enterprise, and everyone will be far happier about the situation.

But that's not "natural," you say? While I'm confessing things, I must further confess that every time I hear someone use the word *natural* in conjunction with women and maternity, I want to rip them limb from limb. *How's that for "natural"?* I'd like to say. *That's* how nature likes it—brutal, painful, and capricious. So please shut up about nature already.

A THOUSAND OTHER THINGS

by

Kate Christensen

I DON'T HAVE KIDS, and I'm very glad I don't, although there was a time when I wanted them more than anything.

These days, I live in a nineteenth-century brick house in the gritty, beautiful, easygoing seaside town of Portland, Maine, with my boyfriend of almost six years, Brendan, and our sweet old dog, Dingo. Brendan is thirty-two; I'm almost fifty-two. Despite or maybe because of our age difference, we're deeply happy and contented in the way of best friends who can't bear to be apart and yet maintain an inextinguishable spark of mutual attraction.

This isn't a life I thought I would ever have, especially ten or fifteen years ago—not even close. Back then, I thought I'd never leave New York; I was embedded in a long-term marriage, and believed that I was past any major upheaval.

But if I've learned anything, it's that nothing is permanent. Everything can change unexpectedly, and it's a good idea never to get too complacent. My childhood was marked by change and loss, as was my adolescence; my father abandoned my sisters and me when we were young, and our lives were peripatetic, marked by saying good-bye to people every year or two and starting over in new schools, houses, neighborhoods. My adulthood has followed suit; this seems to be a major theme in my life. Brendan and I are both writers, so our income varies wildly from year to year. Sometimes we're broke, sometimes flush, usually somewhere in between. We're glad not to have to worry about supporting anyone but ourselves. We lavish our caretaking energies on each other and Dingo, and that's all we seem to require.

Brendan has never wanted kids, and I believe he never will; he knows himself very well. He has no desire to be a father, no interest in having a family. Seeing other people with their kids, no matter how cute they are, only reinforces his knowledge that he doesn't want them. That I don't want them either is probably moot by now, since I'm likely too old to conceive. But it's not over till it's over. And so we're careful.

Years ago, when my then husband and I were in our mid-thirties, we'd been married for two years and I felt forty approaching fast. We had weathered our rocky first years together. Our marriage finally felt stable and solid. We'd had a wild, carefree, decadent four years of courtship and early marriage, and now that we were getting older, it felt like time to settle down, or at least it did for me. And on top of it, my best friend and sister were both pregnant.

Suddenly, I had baby lust: deep, primal, a shockingly animal yearning I'd never experienced before. It was like being on some weird and powerful new drug. I could feel my baby in my arms; a girl, I imagined. I could see myself becoming a mother. I longed for the tectonic shifts motherhood would bring. I fantasized about nursing her, rocking her to sleep, leaping out of bed in the night when she cried. I craved that sense of importance and completion, the passionate focus on something outside myself. All my life, I had assumed I'd have kids, and now it was time: I was ready.

The fact that my husband didn't have these feelings at all, didn't remotely share my excitement about settling down and growing up and changing our lives, came as a further shock. But I wasn't deterred. Frankly, it felt like my decision to make, unilaterally, as the wife. Didn't wives always tell their husbands when it was time? Wasn't that how this was supposed to go? And didn't husbands give in, reluctantly, then fall madly in love with their children and rise to the role of fathering and never regret a thing?

My father, for one, hadn't. After abandoning twin baby girls in Minnesota, moving to California, and marrying my much-younger mother, he'd fathered three more daughters he apparently didn't want. My mother has conjectured that if one of us had been a boy, this story, and his relationship with us, might have gone differently, but that is moot. He was a negligent, distant, sometimes violent, often heartbreakingly charming father who disappeared forever when we were all still little, along with the child support he'd provided. He'd once told my teenage sister, "When you were little and you'd yell, 'Daddy, Daddy!' I'd look around to see who that person was. Then I realized it was me. I've just never felt like that guy."

But I'd married my husband, in part, because I knew he could and would be a good father, even a great one. I'd watched him hold a friend's baby on our third date, cradling its head, rocking it gently, not missing a beat in his conversation. He was a natural. I thought then, *I could marry this man.* By which I meant I could have children with this man.

But the script I'd written in my head went off course. No matter how much I begged and pleaded and raged and wept for more than a year, my husband adamantly refused to have children. He wasn't ready to give up his youth, all the fun we were having, the freedom to spend all day in his studio and come home late for dinner and be alone with me at night and travel wherever we wanted, to Mexico, New Orleans, Amsterdam.

He was a musician, photographer, and painter. I was a novelist. I'd finally sold my first novel and was working on my second. But he was struggling to get a show, to market the album his band had produced. Our careers were in different places. I suspect that if they'd been more equal, he might have been willing to have children when I was ready, but again, as with my father, this is all moot.

A few years later, he finally decided that he was ready to

have kids. I was forty by then. I was also no longer happy in the marriage, no longer filled with much optimism about it, in part because of his earlier refusal to have children with me, which had broken my heart irreparably. Along the way, my baby lust had abated along with my lust for my husband, and I now felt somewhat ambivalent about the whole question. Still, I was willing, and he was ready. I had said I wanted a baby—two, actually—and I still trusted the authenticity of my earlier yearning. I also trusted that once I had a baby in my arms, once I was a mother, I would embrace the role and never look back.

So we started trying. I stopped drinking alcohol, started taking prenatal vitamins. Then my period, which had never been late in my life, was a few days late, then a week, then ten days. My breasts were incredibly, horribly sore. I felt different—puffy, muted, muffled. I scheduled a visit to my gynecologist, and then I bought a pregnancy test from the drugstore. The result was negative, but maybe it was too early.

My husband, once he realized I might be pregnant, seemed calm, even joyful and excited. He seemed ready to be a father, and I had no doubt about his abilities or commitment. I knew that he would never abandon our child or children. I knew that he would do everything in his power to make sure they were loved, safe, fed, educated, taken care of. He would be the devoted father I hadn't had. I had done that, at least, for my baby.

But what kind of mother was this kid getting?

As I later realized, I was at the beginning of what turned

out to be a sort of protracted nervous breakdown that lasted into my mid-forties, until just after I left my husband and moved out of our house. Before this pregnancy, or whatever it was, I had been suffering from out-of-control, despairing crying jags during which I could hardly get out of bed, alternating with manic episodes that involved inappropriate flirting, heavy drinking, and staying up all night, playing online Scrabble and obsessing about aging, mortality, and death.

The irony of having a new life inside me during this episode was not lost on me.

My mother, too, had experienced a long breakdown in her forties. I knew that being a mother had in no way made this easier for her. In fact, because of it, she'd been unable to provide her adolescent daughters the strong-minded guidance and nurturing attention she'd wanted to give us. She couldn't escape the storms raging in her own skull any more than I was now able to escape mine. I worried that if I had a baby, I'd inflict this on her. I would be a good mother in every way I could, but I'd also be a very troubled one.

I'd heard other women exult about the magic of being pregnant, the glow of it, the joy and anticipation. I'd expected a sense of completion, fulfillment, the romantic thrill of doing what my body was designed and meant to do. I felt some of that in bursts, but my ambivalence continued unabated. I also felt terrified, displaced. I went around all day with gingerly trepidation, nervous and baffled and neurotic, trying not to inhale truck exhaust, jonesing for a glass of wine, feeling my normally robust sexuality withering into bodily caution, anxiousness about my ability to properly house this interloper for whom I would have done anything, killed anyone, to shield from harm. I was, it seemed, biologically programmed to feel this way. I had no choice.

At night, I lay awake, trying not to feel trapped, invaded, hijacked by this thing inside me, this rapidly growing person who was simultaneously independent of me, entitled to me, wholly dependent on me, and part of me. My body, which all my life had been my own, inhabited solely by me, free to do whatever it wanted, now felt entirely given over to the task of growing this stranger. All of my choices about what I put into it and what I did with it were made wholly with this other person in mind, no longer myself. Sometimes I was excited. Other times, I was freaked-out. But even as I vacillated, I accepted all of this as a permanent change. I'd never be wholly autonomous again. That's what motherhood was, in a nutshell.

Then, the very morning of my OB-GYN appointment, I started to bleed, more heavily than usual. Just like that, my pregnancy, if it really had been a pregnancy, was over. I was flooded with relief, mad with it. I felt some sadness, a twinge of loss, but primarily, I was exultant and grateful. I celebrated by going out with my husband and some of our friends and drinking tequila, smoking cigarettes, and staying out till dawn.

Now, it turned out, I was the one who didn't want to give

up this life of carefree independence. My husband's reaction seemed more complex: part relief, part sadness. I sensed that he had been scared, too, but he'd been more ready than I was.

Despite a lot of carelessness with birth control in my youth, this was the first time I'd thought I was pregnant. Once it was over, I understood that I'd been saved from losing myself. My earlier desire for babies, now gone, felt like a phantom echo of a lost passion, a heartbreak long ago recovered from. I threw myself back into my own life, greeting all my old depression, mania, bad behavior, and obsessiveness as if they were friends I'd neglected and almost lost. I hadn't known how much I treasured them.

A year or two later, my gynecologist announced that my fibroids had to come out. One was the size of a cantaloupe, another a grapefruit, a third an orange. Luckily, all these benign flesh fruits were growing outside my uterus. They didn't cause me pain and could be easily removed, but the biggest one was pressing on my bladder, and when I lay on my back, I could see the rounded top of it poking up through my skin. So we scheduled a traditional C-section-like operation.

Of course I spent the night before the surgery on the Internet, googling laparoscopic procedures, which have a far faster recovery time and leave a tiny scar instead of a six-inch one. The next morning, I called my doctor, furious we weren't doing it that way. He countered that the fibroids were too big and told me not to spend the night on Google before an operation; he also postponed the surgery until my state of mind improved.

About a month later, I had the operation. Afterward, I was sent to recuperate for a couple of days on the maternity ward of St. Vincent's. I shared a room with a woman a little older than I was who'd just had a radical hysterectomy. We were the only two on the ward who'd come in for an operation, without a baby, with pieces of ourselves missing. We bonded deeply over this; she had kids already, but she understood my own feelings about the matter.

I had become hugely bloated after my operation and had gained more than twenty extra pounds of water weight, which made me feel like an enormous, lumbering freak. It seemed monstrously unfair that I'd just had a few pounds of flesh taken out of me and had instantly become too fat to fit into my clothes. And it felt ironic: my body seemed to be revolting against the invasion that had just taken place, insulating itself with a thick layer of protective water. With my distended stomach, I felt nine months pregnant. My newly stitched incision was tender and painful from the pressure.

When it was time to go home, I put on the shapeless, baggy dress I'd asked my husband to bring me, the only article of clothing I owned that would fit. He helped me dress and pack. Weak as I felt, I skirted the nurses' station so I wouldn't have to ride out in a wheelchair; I needed to get out of there under my own steam. I leaned against my husband, and he carried my bag and opened the hallway door for me.

Then something happened, something that has stayed with me ever since. As we went through the swinging hall door to the elevator bay, my husband looked back and saw a beatific young woman approaching, carrying a newborn baby and surrounded by an entourage. She was too far away for him to be expected to keep the door open for her and her husband, mother, and friend, so he let it close and pressed the button for the elevator.

A minute later the woman sailed through the door, which her own husband held open for her. They all joined us in the hallway.

"You could have held the door open for me," she said to my husband.

Shocked, I stared at her. She was beautiful and tiny, with long, curly dark hair. She wore a gauzy skirt and sandals and looked as if she'd already lost all her pregnancy weight, or maybe she'd magically transferred it to me somehow.

My husband, as shocked as I was, didn't answer. We rode the elevator down in silence. The doors opened on the ground floor. I waited in the lobby for my husband to bring the car around, leaning heavily against a planter and watching this new mother allow everyone to pamper her in any way they could.

Her husband looked over at me. He could have been one of my husband's cousins, kindly, Jewish, concerned. "Are you okay?" he asked me.

I almost burst into tears. I was flooded with sadness. Two days on the maternity ward with a C-section incision but no baby, followed by an elevator ride with a gorgeous, doted-upon Madonna holding her beautiful bundle, had hit me hard out of nowhere. I went home in tears. My husband couldn't console me.

A few years later, in the fall of 2006, I moved out of our Greenpoint, Brooklyn, house into a basement in Hunter's Point, Queens. I had just ended a devastating, short-lived affair with a married man who lived in our neighborhood, a college friend of my husband's, probably the worst person I could have chosen. The affair was over; I couldn't speak to him or contact him, and I didn't, ever again. I knew I'd done a terrible thing, as had he, and my guilt and regret exacerbated the wrenching and painful and devastating aftermath of the affair. I lay awake in my dungeon apartment night after night. I could not sleep. I was in a state of manic existential despair so profound, so all-encompassing, it drove me to what I now recognize as actual insanity. I had left my husband, the person I loved and trusted most, because our marriage had become intolerable to me. Although he was willing to take me back and work it out and although I wanted more than anything to stay married to him, I had to go. I was propelled out of our house by an instinctive, self-protective urge to flee. And I had lost my lover, whom I was madly in love with and who I believed at the time was my soul mate, because he had kids and I couldn't take him away from them, and he couldn't leave them.

Wracked with guilt and horror at myself and filled with

painful, insoluble feelings, I lay awake too desolate to cry. I stared into the darkness for all the hours of the night. My skull echoed with one question: *Where are my children?*

The whole summer before, I'd experienced a strange reprisal of my old mourning for the babies I'd never had. I'd thought I had recovered for good from that sadness, but as I felt my marriage disintegrate, the memory of my raw yearning for babies and my husband's refusal to have them with me came back to me as part of the reason I was now leaving him. It felt like the heart of why I was so lonely with him. As I lay awake in the Hunter's Point basement every night, that old unfulfilled craving became an obsession I couldn't escape, a black hole of raw grief I kept falling deeper into. *Where are my children?* I felt their absence and loss as if they existed somewhere I couldn't reach, as if they were stuck forever on the other side of a membrane and I could never have access to them. I felt as if they were real. I knew it was part of my current psychosis, a hallucination in 3-D, but knowing this didn't help at all. I missed my children desperately.

The part of me that had wanted to be a mother all those years ago had woken up again, and she was howling and keening like a tragic heroine at the end of an opera. Gradually, I pulled myself out of the abyss. In the next months, I finished a novel. In December, unable to bear my loneliness, I went back to my husband and stayed for another two years. We saw a marital therapist once a week. We tried so hard to work it out, but in the end, it wasn't meant to be, at least not for me. The therapy helped clarify for me that I truly couldn't stay in this marriage, and I truly didn't want kids.

When I left for good in the fall of 2008, it was with sadness and grief, but also resolve and finality, and not one twinge of longing for children.

Since then, my life has swept on without them, and other passions and experiences and sources of love have gradually taken up my energy and attention. There was, and still is, no void where they would have been. In fact, I have no room in my life for kids, no place for them, no time.

I remember my long-ago feverish urge to have a baby fondly and with relief. It seems to me, in hindsight, that it was a biological, hormonal impulse, an imperative that arose when the right moment came and then, unfulfilled, simply went away over time. If I had had children with my ex-husband, I would have had to choose between staying in a marriage that was unsatisfying and lonely and leaving and breaking up my family and sharing custody with my ex-husband, negotiating everyone's schedule for many years. Instead of being autonomous and traveling light, I would have had a hard time leaving New York and separating my kids from their father. I might have been stuck there, too. I might never have met Brendan, never moved north to the White Mountains and Maine. I would have missed out on so much.

I picture my life without children as a hole dug in sand and then filled with water. Into every void rushes something. Nature abhors a vacuum. Into the available space and time and energy of my kid-free life rushed a thousand other things. I published seven books in fourteen years and am writing two more now; I've written countless essays, interviews, reviews, blog posts, e-mails. My days are so busy and full and yet so calm and uninterrupted and self-directed, I can't imagine how kids would fit in. Kids talk so much. They require their parents' undivided attention on demand. They are expensive. They require oceans of energy and attention. And so forth. No matter how much you love your kids, they're always there, and you are entirely responsible for them, and this goes on for many, many years. Meanwhile, I'm an introvert and so is Brendan. Children exhaust us, even the ones we love most. Our solitude is the most valuable thing we have, and we cherish it above most other things and work hard to maintain it.

Sometimes we posit a scenario in which we were both young when we met, and we imagine that we would have had kids, if only because I would have wanted them. And we would have raised them with all our best efforts and unflagging commitment. But we also would have become different people, made different choices, and had a different relationship with each other; more distant and harried, more responsible, more grown-up.

Instead, we have this life, and we are these people. We get to go to bed every night together, alone, and wake up together, alone. Our shared passions thrill and satisfy us, and our abundant freedoms—to daydream; to cook exactly the food we want when we want it; to drink wine and watch a movie without worrying about who's not yet asleep upstairs; to pick up and go anywhere we want, anytime; to do our work uninterrupted; to shape our own days to our own liking; and to stay connected to each other without feeling fractured— are not things we'd choose to give up for anyone, ever.

Meanwhile, there are a lot of kids in my life. I have six nieces and nephews and I am the godmother of my best friend's son and daughter. But most of my friends do not have kids; I am part of a community of childless people, many of them single, most of them artists of some stripe. Not having kids is the norm for my friends and for me. We get together and find we have plenty to talk about and no one to interrupt us.

I attribute my present-day happiness to sheer luck. I didn't choose not to have kids, it just happened to me—my husband didn't want them when I did, and then when he did, we weren't able to have them.

Since that terrible fall of 2006, I've never wanted them again. During those long nights I spent lying awake dying of loneliness and pining for them, I think I said good-bye to them forever. I let them go back to the void, those unknown people I would have loved with all my heart and soul but will never know. I can't miss what I've never had.

THE NEW RHODA

by

Paul Lisicky

(1) I KNEW THE SONG, knew the dreamy leaps of the singer's voice, but I couldn't place its name. I couldn't remember where or when I knew it, but the song felt like a sign now, a little wonder I needed to be responsible to. It wasn't so much the words—I rarely care about the words; a good song alchemizes sense into pure sound—but the atmosphere, its three key changes, which felt distilled rather than willed into being. How had I lost the song? If I continued to sit still, if I didn't attend to this need to place it, I wouldn't have the song to return to again. In a little bit I wouldn't even remember that the song was something to miss, and if I could be that kind of casual about beautiful things, then why bother trying to write anymore? I know I was probably making too big a deal about this. It was the Fourth of July, Philadelphia.

I was sitting in the empty coffee place around the corner from my new apartment.

I could have asked the barista. I could have said, *Hey, what's this band?* But I didn't want to let on that I actually listened to music like this. To let on would be to expose myself. To admit that I don't always act my age and know things a twenty-three-year-old might know. An old guy poking around where his nose isn't supposed to be, or worse, a showoff. I did not want to chance being condescended to. It seemed preferable—safer, really—to keep my not-knowing private even at the expense of losing the song. This was music made by and for the young, not for someone who had grown up listening to the Smiths and buying LPs and cassette tapes at record stores. I was likely the same age as the barista's father—probably I was even older than his father—and the fact that my life was so far outside the usual paradigms made me feel unexpectedly—what? *Raw.* It wasn't that I wanted to be a father. It wasn't that I was bemoaning a life I could have had—nothing so typical as that. My not being a father had kept me young, had kept my curiosity awake. It was indeed possible to opt out of growing up, if by growing up we mean shutting down our interest in the next or the new. I didn't have to restrict myself to the behaviors of some role. But not everyone wants to know that. It could be dangerous news, even to a young bearded barista who might just be feeling territorial about the music he plays.

(2) In a not-so-distant past, men like me often died in their twenties and thirties. We continued to do what men like us had always done, and though the sex we had was called "safe," the sex itself felt like a pact with a grenade. The grenade might not go off right away, but in five years it might blow up in your face, scorching your retinas, while you were out having a peaceful dinner. We were either worried all the time or entirely numb to our worry. A friend of a friend told the story of a man who gargled with grapefruit juice before deciding to go out on Saturday nights. If he felt the slightest sting inside his mouth (maybe a nick from the toothbrush the night before, a bit lip), he'd rinse with water immediately, reach for a book, and spend the night at home, thus preempting the idea of sex in a less than tip-top state, which for him lay too close to the possibility of seroconversion.

This was not exactly a crazy man. Or, I should say, he was no crazier than the rest of us.

Meanwhile, another world went on around us. People in that world bought life insurance, health insurance, houses, summer property to be passed on to children, grandchildren. They weren't exactly in the here and now. They were busy turning to some future, but what is the future when you are always feeding it money? Doesn't it get tiring to give so much away to a world that you'll never get to touch and see?

All my men had was the here and now, which often meant staying out half the night, dancing or standing in front of speakers that buzzed so loudly they hurt our ears. Inside the nightclub hung an oversized replica of an AZT capsule suspended with black wires from the ceiling. It glittered in the hot air, blue band down the center, like some icon we'd conjured up together. The title of the theme night was appropriately irreverent (the name escapes me now), for how could anyone be anything but irreverent about a drug that gave half the people in the room rashes, chills, dizziness, nausea, swelling of the tongue? What do you have when you don't have a future? You have gallows humor, which, as it turns out, does a pretty good job of turning tinfoil into platinum. The last thing we were thinking about was children, or being parents. We were still children ourselves, though we might have been doctors, professors, caregivers, counselors. A reclaimed childhood was not something to waste—we knew that much—having spent so much of our actual own childhoods repressed, depressed, waiting to get out. Nor was it escape.

(3) Imagine it. Look at a drop of your blood, your semen, your saliva, and think of it containing a thousand little grenades. Not just for you, but for the lover you came into intimate contact with. How would your life change? Could you ever disappear into yourself, your skin again? When you finally got the nerve to be tested, and found out that you did not carry those grenades, could you still think of that fluid as a substance you'd choose to make a baby with? Imagine it.

One does not feel exactly undead after being dead for so long.

---

(4) Not so long ago, my friend Dawn asked what it was like to grow up in that time. We were talking about the idea of children, after watching two younger daddies pushing a stroller by our sidewalk café. The evening was arid, windy. A sudden gust lifted the cocktail napkin from the table. I dashed after it and almost caught it before it sailed off over the hood of the car. My ability to explain that era felt a little like that escaped napkin—or was it the gust? My language felt too small for me to contain it. I tried my best to say it my way, through my metaphors, not the ones that have already been branded into us by way of the usual narratives. But the more I talked, the more I focused on Dawn's face, which was loving, pitying, uncomprehending. She was trying so hard to understand; I could feel her working, and I hated the distance my fumbling opened up between us.

(5) Not every man of that time was caught in the same fog. There were R and J, for example, who had been together since they were undergraduate roommates at Harvard. They professed to having slept with no one but each other. I'm not sure that meant that their sex lives were any wilder than anyone else's, but to make love to each other without the threat of caution, precaution—it was just unimaginable to me. Futurity for them had to be different from futurity for me. The same could also have been said about N and O, monogamous for twenty-two years. When they talked about having a child with a surrogate mother, I was as disoriented as if they were talking about fusing a goat with a hen. Gay men in the 1990s

were just not doing that yet. It was still unheard of, and when M, my ex, and I talked about their plan, we couldn't help wondering whether it was corrupt, a doomed attempt to please some needy parents. And so much money—couldn't they be giving money like that to the poor, to animals? Men like us were supposed to be utopians; men like us were supposed to be reinventing the future, even if there wasn't exactly a future to inhabit. M and I talked about them with bewildered faces, both superior and a little sorry for them, as if they'd somehow missed the obvious answer to the quiz. We thought of them as if they weren't members of the tribe. We talked about them as if they were little old ladies. Obviously sex did not matter enough to them. Somehow they got stunted along the way and were too afraid of what lay ahead for them. They should have been wearing lumberjack shirts. They should have been taking their protein powders, working out, making their bodies massive with shoulder shrugs. Were they not looking around? It was time to get busy, investing in the business of looking healthy, healthy, healthy.

(6) Did A sense how rare and valuable she was to N and O? Did she manage to turn the intensity of their love—she'd become the sole project of her parents' relationship—into pressure? Did she feel she had to be better, smarter, brighter than the other kids in her preschool? Did she have to be cute just one more time for her parents' friends? Maybe that explained why A was unbearable, almost comically unbearable, whenever her parents took her out on the town. She threw tan-

trums; she scratched and grabbed and spit out the sauce on her pasta. Once, from the other side of the restaurant, we watched her parents pick up the pieces of the teacup she'd slammed against the chair. M and I took to referring to her as the New Rhoda, for the evil child played by Patty Mc-Cormack in *The Bad Seed*. The stories we made up about her turned out to be parables about the folly of parents taking on a role they weren't meant to take on. In these stories, everyone played the expected parts—the exasperated, embarrassed parents and the self-righteous, fussy acquaintances—while the New Rhoda bombed cemeteries, tore up trees, knocked toothless old men off their crutches.

(7) Treatments change, lives change, and though the world still looks pretty much the same, it isn't the same at all. People who think they have six months to live end up thriving twenty years later. These days there's even a drug you can take to prevent seroconversion. I like to think I'm not a person who's welded to my generation. I like to think that the full range of my character is available to me, simultaneously, at any moment: the me I was, the me I'll be. But in crucial ways, I'll always be someone wired by growing up during that siege.

So maybe that's why choosing a child (or not, for that matter) feels like an incredible luxury. As soon as I entertain the question, a door opens, and I'm too flooded to think. How many other choices have I not considered because it seemed that they weren't mine to make? What have I accommodated and settled for simply because I came into adulthood in a dark, alarming time? It is easier than you think to be indifferent to what you've been told you can't have. People do it all over the world, all the time, for reasons that are usually imposed on them. As soon as I stare through that open door, I want to close it right away. There isn't any point in feeling defeated by the empty room inside. I'd rather keep building the house I've already been building, even if it's crooked, faded at the roof, with a cracked foundation.

(8) Why, Child-Who-Never-Was, am I feeling a little down as I assemble these thoughts? I never thought that you were someone to miss until I began looking at the empty chair where you might have sat. Who would you have been? Would you have had big ears like me, big nose, big head? Would you have had my long feet? Would you have been a loner one day and a social person the next, the guy who loved the party so much that he'd be the last to say good night? Would you have loved animals? What about music? The sea—would you have wanted to be near it, in it, and evaluated every place in terms of how many miles it was from the water? Would you have carried my essence forward in ways I couldn't have known? Would you have taught me how to ski or to care about football or to make a devil's food cake from scratch?

(9) When my relationship of sixteen years ended, I left New York for the Nearby State, where it soon became clear that you were considered odd if you went to a restaurant or a movie

THE NEW RHODA | 71

by yourself. I'm talking about the subtlest signals: facial reactions from a waitress instead of anything spoken. Solitary
men were a special cause for concern, their aloneness the outward sign of a hex. I couldn't help but wonder whether
people chose to have families to avoid some stranger's inscru-
table projection. If the desire to have children is just a way to
build some noisy tribe of distraction around oneself, then I'd
rather be alone.

(10) On a foggy spring night in Provincetown, I'm sitting in
a bar with three straight friends: two men, one woman. We
are celebrating I's fortieth birthday, and he is here—though
he didn't come out and say this—because he didn't want to
spend it alone. He is not so many months out of a breakup,
so he drove fourteen hours and nine hundred miles to spend
it in a place that he loves. Though we are laughing and on
our second round, the evening is saturated with the possibility of melancholy. Aloneness is the unspoken story of the
evening. Time, too. I'm looking up at the portraits of lost
local fishermen over the window; the dash and flair of each
sketch gives each fellow the aura of a 1980s art star.

I don't know how the conversation gets around to the dif-
ferences between how men and women age, but U talks with
determined frustration about the fact that men have more
years than women do. By that she doesn't mean longer lives—
statistics tell us that that isn't true, of course—but a longer
time to be fertile, desirable.

L and I mention that they're attracted to women younger

than they are because, yes, they still want to be fathers, and they could never expect such fertility of anyone their own age.

Their response makes U's eyes smolder, but quietly. The left corner of her mouth turns down. This is not what she wants to hear. Maybe she was hoping that one of us would say this idea is full of shit; men and women are not so radically different after all and it's never so useful to make generalizations like that.

The potential conversation that this topic provokes is so combustible it is collectively cut off. We are here to have fun. We are smart enough to see that this subject might have the power to burn up the night. And we couldn't do that on I's birthday. We order a third round.

As for me? I make a joke about not knowing what they are talking about. My manner of delivery makes everyone laugh, but I'm masking a deeper confusion. I thought I could imagine what it could be like to be in my straight male friends' skin, to be swept and stopped by some beautiful woman as she walks down the street. But the sexual allure of reproductivity? Really? Could they be serious, or are they just reproducing what their fathers might have said, back when they were kids?

I've never felt more alien from the men I thought I'd known.

We say our good nights. We walk out into the mists of Commercial Street. On my walk back to my studio, I pass some intense-faced guy with thick brows and a full beard right out of the nineteenth century. I turn around and check out his hard butt as he walks past a tumble of roses. Imagine, wanting to get to know him for the width of his hips, the dream of the little wet monkey growing inside him!

(11) My questions lead back to the mother, my mother. Did she even want to be a parent? Well, she had to, on some level, though I imagine she would have preferred to be our friend. The only thing I can truly remember her wanting in her life— aside from the house in Seven Hills, and maybe an Ethan Allen living room set—was a girl. This was years after my brother Bobby and I had come along. She'd talked about this girl so much that Bobby rebelled by saying he wanted a duck. The more he wanted a duck, the more my mother wanted Diane Michelle, the name she'd given to the baby growing inside her. Diane Michelle accumulated pink: a pink baby blanket, a pink mobile above the crib, a mound of pink toys. But when Diane Michelle turned out to have a penis in the delivery room, my mother broke down and cried for a couple of days. She adored Michael after those couple of days passed, but we always had the sense that boys weren't her first love and we could never give her what she'd wanted. "I used to have long eyelashes before I had you kids," she said more than once. Troubling words, part fairy tale, part fever dream, spoken in the voice of sweet disappointment. For years I couldn't get that picture out of my head: our once beautiful mother, ruined by us, her eyelashes eaten away by the acids of her body.

(12) When she was alive, I distinctly remember pressures from my mother: the pressure to go to college, the pressure

to do well in college, to make money, to be a doctor or a lawyer. Strangely, there was never any pressure to have children. I'm not just talking about my mother here, but my father, too. Perhaps they wanted us all to themselves. Perhaps if we were parents, we'd no longer be just their children, and they'd be one step further from being children themselves, an honor they probably weren't willing to give up just yet. Honestly, I think they would have been happy for us to live on in our childhood bedrooms until we were well into our forties and beyond. My mother seemed to know that children were only meant to be lost, and once she felt us pulling away from her, she pulled away, too. Yet she burst into tears whenever I stood by my packed car on the driveway, ready to leave for another semester. She behaved as if there had always been the One Great Leaving and each iteration of it brought the same welling up. A love that big could only create havoc, and I hurried out of her arms, ashamed to be the one who could stir her up like that.

When Michael brought his baby daughter to meet her for the first time, it was assumed she'd finally get her Diane Michelle—or at least the New Diane Michelle. I'm sure she was delighted to hold Jordan close to her, as Michael stood watching, smiling, waiting to bask in her approval, but she handed the baby back to him a little sooner than he expected. By then she was losing herself: parts of her language, parts of her memory. The old idea of manners was gone. She'd already had enough of children. And, more often than not, she understood herself as a child: "Where's my mother?"

she'd say. "Where did she go? Have you seen her?" On the dining room table sat Jordan's presents. My mother's eyes drifted over to the pink-wrapped boxes, as if she'd just decided it was *her* birthday and wasn't it time to tear one open?

(13) In spite of my doubts, I'd probably say yes if I ever became involved with someone who wanted to be a parent. I'm not saying that lightly, though I might be saying it with the same level of commitment with which I'd say, "Of course I'd move to Tokyo." How do we even talk about the future when there's less and less of it every minute? Who are we kidding when we speak of planning the time ahead? So I'll just talk to the Child-Who-Might-Never-Be instead: It is too late for me to be the kind of parent you might want. I will not be like the parents of your friends. I will probably hang out with your friends, and when they come to the house to visit, they'll probably want to see me as much as they want to see you. My mother was just like that, remember? We will squeeze chocolate syrup onto our yogurt. We will take the stereo out into the backyard and turn up the volume too loud, disturbing the next-door neighbors. We will name the birds in the branches and on the lawn: song sparrow, house finch, marsh wren, cardinal. I will probably embarrass you by the way I dress. (*Skinny jeans again? Dad!*) No, I will not put on another pair of pants. You will get used to my awkwardness, my kisses, my dropped keys, my trying to be present with you, now and now and now and now.

BE HERE NOW MEANS
BE GONE LATER

by

Lionel Shriver

MEET THE ANTIMOM. When my seventh novel, *We Need to Talk About Kevin*, became a best seller in 2005, the story it told—about motherhood gone dreadfully wrong—drew fire from Catholic web pages for being hostile to "family." Meanwhile, grotesque distortions of the book's underlying theme (such as, "It's all right to hate your own child, and if they turn out badly it's not your fault") spoored from article to article like potato blight. Devastated mothers sent me confiding handwritten letters detailing horror stories of hideous tyros just like the boy in my book. Women who'd declined to have children clamored to my readings, raising the novel high as proof that they were right. I earned my own little chapter in Nicki Defago's *Childfree and Loving It!*

Yet by the time *Kevin* won the Orange Prize that year, when my role as poster girl for "maternal ambivalence" was jacked up to yet another power, something strange had started to happen. I sometimes departed from the script. When a London *Sunday Times* reporter (who clearly thought me a chilly, typically arrogant American bitch) asked if I didn't think that declining to reproduce wasn't essentially "nihilistic," I said readily, "Of course." Or a journalist would ask tentatively on a phoner: Wasn't refusing parenthood a little . . . selfish? I'd cry boisterously into the receiver, "Absolutely!"

The truth is, I had started to feel guilty.

Childless at fifty-seven, I'm old enough for the question of motherhood to have become purely philosophical. But during my reproductive years, I had all the time in the world to have babies. I maintained two consecutive long-term relationships, one a marriage that continues to thrive. I was in perfect health. I could have afforded children, financially. I just didn't want them. They are untidy; they would have messed up my apartment. In the main, they are ungrateful. They would have siphoned too much time away from the writing of my precious books.

Nevertheless, after talking myself blue about "maternal ambivalence," I came full circle, rounding on the advice to do as I say, not as I did. I may not, for my own evil purposes, regret giving motherhood a miss, but I long ago wearied of being the Antimom, and would gladly hand the part to someone else. For anyone who's interested, I have a T-shirt of an infant with a big red slash through it that's going cheap.

Allusion to the West's "aging population" in the news is commonplace. We have more and more old people, and a dwindling number of young people to support them. Not only health care and pension systems but the working young could soon be overtaxed, just to keep doddering crusties like Lionel Shriver stocked with Depends. Politicians sensibly cite age structure to justify higher rates of immigration. Long periods of look-the-other-way policing of American borders have indeed left the United States with an economically healthier age structure than we would have today without waves of young immigrants and their larger families.

Yet curiously little heed is paid to *why* the West is aging. Our gathering senescence is routinely referenced like an inexorable force of nature, a process beyond our control, like the shifting of tectonic plates or the ravages of a hurricane. To the contrary, age structure is profoundly within human control. Remarkably resistant to governmental manipulation, it is the sum total of millions of single, deeply private decisions by people like me and a startlingly large proportion of my friends and acquaintances.

We haven't had kids.

Western fertility started to dive in the 1970s—the same era in which, ironically, alarmist population guru Paul

Ehrlich was predicting that we would all soon be balancing on our one square foot of earth per person, like angels on the head of a pin. Numerous factors have contributed to the Incredible Shrinking Family: the introduction of reliable contraception, the wholesale entry of women into the workforce, delayed parenthood and thus higher infertility, the fact that children no longer till your fields but expect your help in putting a down payment on a massive mortgage.

Yet I believe all of these contributing elements may be subsidiary to a larger transformation in Western culture no less profound than our collective consensus on what life is for.

Statistics are never boring if you can see through the numbers to what they mean, so bear with me. The Total Fertility Rate is the number of children the average woman will bear over her lifetime. Allowing for infant mortality, the TFR required to maintain a population at its current size is 2.1. In 2013, American women had an average TFR of 1.9—a rate modestly below replacement. Many years could pass before that deficit will make itself felt.

Thus Jonathan Last's provocative 2013 book, *What to Expect When No One's Expecting: America's Coming Demographic Disaster*, is either disingenuous or off the beam. Americans are not about to die out. According to UN estimates, from 316 million in 2013, the U.S. population is likely to grow to 448 million by mid-century—although a massive whack of that growth is to result from immigration.

If hardly an endangered species, one population in the

United States *is* contracting: white people. Politically awkward, yes, which is why Mr. Last's alarm about low birthrates among "Americans" is a cover for his real alarm: about feeble fertility among people who look like him and me. As of 2010, white American women had a TFR of 1.79—a figure that might not sound terribly low, but one that has remained in that well-below-replacement-rate ballpark since at least 1980. Cumulatively, that shortfall has consequences. By 2043, whites will constitute a minority in the United States, while Hispanics, whose TFR is now a healthy 2.35 and was for decades closer to 3.0, will go from being one in six Americans to one in three. Liberally minded white Americans are not supposed to care. And I'm not claiming here that you have to care.

Even more striking are the figures in Europe, whence my forebears hail (both sides of my family are German American). Among countries once renowned for their family orientation, Spain has a meager TFR of 1.3, Italy and Greece of 1.4; ditto Germany—where a staggering two-fifths of educated women are having no children whatsoever. The cumulative TFR for all of Europe is only 1.6, expected to translate into a net loss of population by 2050, and that's *including* high levels of immigration. Already by 2000, seventeen European countries were recording more deaths than births. Absent immigration, their populations would be shrinking by now.

Elsewhere, couples still heed the biblical admonition to be fruitful and multiply. Niger has the highest TFR in the world at 7.6. By 2050, the population of Yemen—geograph-ically a little smaller than France—is projected to increase its 1950 population by twenty-four times, exceeding the pop-ulation of Russia. At 3.0 (excluding China), poor nations' TFR is nearly twice that of the wealthier West, and these countries will provide virtually all the extra 3 billion people expected to inhabit our planet by mid-century.

As for what explains the drastic disparity between family size in the West and the rest, sure, we have readier access to contraception. But medical technology is only one piece of the puzzle. During the Industrial Revolution, Western fer-tility rates plunged in a similar fashion. This so-called "de-mographic transition" is usually attributed to the conversion from a rural agrarian economy to an urban industrialized one, and thus to children's shift from financial asset to financial burden. But what is fascinating about the abrupt decrease in family size at the turn of the last century is that it was accom-plished *without the Pill*. Without diaphragms, IUDs, sper-micides, vaginal sponges, estrogen patches, or commercial condoms. Whether through abstinence, backstreet abortion, infanticide, or the rhythm method, people who couldn't af-ford more children didn't have them. Therefore the increased availability of reliable contraception around 1960 no more than partially explains plummeting birthrates thereafter. The difference between Germany and Niger isn't pharmaceutical; it's cultural.

I propose that we have now experienced a second demo-graphic transition, which cannot be attributed to economics. In both America and Europe the engine driving the "birth dearth" among white, educated elites is existential.

To be ridiculously sweeping: baby boomers and their offspring have shifted emphasis from the communal to the individual, from the future to the present, from virtue to personal satisfaction. Increasingly secular, we pledge allegiance to lowercase gods of our private devising. We are concerned with leading less *a* good life than *the* good life. In contrast to our predecessors, we seldom ask ourselves whether we serve a greater social purpose; we are more likely to ask ourselves if we are happy. We shun self-sacrifice and duty as the soft spots of suckers. We give little thought to the perpetuation of lineage, culture, or nation; we take our heritage for granted. We are ahistorical. We measure the value of our lives within the brackets of our own births and deaths, and we're not especially bothered with what happens once we're dead. As we age—oh, so reluctantly!—we are apt to look back on our pasts and question not did I serve family, God, and country, but did I ever get to Cuba, or run a marathon? Did I take up landscape painting? Was I fat? We will assess the success of our lives in accordance not with whether they were righteous, but with whether they were interesting and fun.

If that package sounds like one big moral step backward, the Be Here Now mentality that has converted from sixties catchphrase to entrenched gestalt has its upsides. There has to be some value in living for today, since at any given time today is all you've got. We justly cherish characters capable of living "in the moment"—or, as a drummer might say, "in the pocket." We admire go-getters determined to pack their lives with as much various experience as time and money provide, who never stop learning, engaging, and savoring what every day offers—in contrast to dour killjoys who are bitter and begrudging in the ceaseless fulfillment of obligation. For the role of humble server, helpmate, and facilitator no longer to constitute the sole model of womanhood surely represents progress for which I am personally grateful. Furthermore, prosperity may naturally lead any well-off citizenry to the final frontier: the self, whose borders are as narrow or infinite as we make them.

Yet the biggest social casualty of Be Here Now is children, who have converted from requirement to option, like heated seats for your car. In deciding what in times past never used to be a choice, we don't consider the importance of raising another generation of our own people, however we might choose to define them. The question is whether kids will make us happy.

However rewarding at times, raising children can also be hard, trying, and dull, inevitably ensnaring us in those sucker values of self-sacrifice and duty. The odds of children making you *happier* are surely no better than fifty-fifty. Studies have repeatedly documented that the self-reported "happiness" index is lower among parents than among the childless. Little wonder that so many women like me have taken a hard look at all those diapers, playgroups, and nasty plastic toys and said no, thanks.

To illustrate my existential explanation for the knee-high birthrate among women of European extraction like me, let's look at three other examples, and why they haven't had children. These are all women (whose names have been changed to protect their privacy) whom I personally admire, whose company I treasure, and whose thinking on this and a range of issues I've been able to follow for years, because we all live in London. In a word, they're my friends. Nevertheless, in sufficient aggregate, we are deadly.

Forty-four when I grilled her on these matters, Gabriella is an accomplished journalist who has published three acclaimed nonfiction books on Africa. She is bright, widely traveled, well educated, and physically fetching, with a distinctive acerbity and a candor unusual for her British upbringing. She is half Italian on her mother's side.

Gabriella was negative about childbearing from the get-go: "I was someone who loathed the onset of sexual maturity. Menstruation, pregnancy—all these biological processes that you couldn't control, which caught you unawares and seemed designed to embarrass you in public—felt like a baffling, humiliating negation of my existence as a thinking, reasoning adult." By her twenties, her hostility had hardened. "I remember being astonished to meet contemporaries who had decided to have children within years of leaving university. It seemed utterly nonsensical. Here we were, just emerged from the tedious constraints of a seemingly endless education, financially independent for the first time, tasting our liberties at last, and the first thing they decided to do was to enter the prison of child rearing, with all its boring routines and dreadful responsibilities. Having children in my twenties would have spelled the end of everything I had spent my life working toward and was about to really enjoy: the ability to spend my money the way I wanted, travel where I wanted, choose my partners, live as I wished."

By her late thirties, however, she had misgivings. Friends were having children, and she felt left out. Encountering other people's children, she realized "there were great joys to be had from the process" and that "watching something [*sic*— to nonparents, children are often mistaken for objects] growing and changing each day was also an intellectually intriguing process." Ergo, kids just might be *interesting and fun*. Yet her then partner was an older man averse to parenthood, partially on (sound) medical grounds. At no point did Gabriella's pining for children become a make-or-break matter in her relationship, from which we can construe that the pining was either mild or theoretical. For the most part, "the issue was ignored, avoided, allowed to slide, or used as a bargaining chip when things got difficult." Indeed, when that relationship hit crisis point and her partner did a U-turn on fatherhood, his offer of a family was insufficient to salvage it for Gabriella. Happiness, in this case the romantic variety, trumped motherhood, period.

Thereafter, Gabriella grew resigned that she would not have children. "Could I now cope with the sheer exhaustion of the early sleepless years? Could I accept, as my friends have, that for the first five years I would stop having interesting conversations with adults my own age and settle for glaze-eyed exchanges I've witnessed as an outsider?" No.

When I ask her what she believes redeems her life in the absence of children, her answers are unhesitating. "First, my work. Not in the sense of ambition and earning power (ha-ha), but in the sense that the only imprint I can leave on this earth is my work. My motto, as the years go by, has become that of Voltaire's Candide: 'Il faut cultiver notre jardin.' We need to tend the garden. Do it as well as you can. Writing is my only skill; I apply it to the best of my abilities." Second, "I live for friendships and family. I have friendships that have gone on for so long and have been so close that I suppose they constitute a form of marriage."

On her own account, she has no regrets. "Had I had children, I would have written no books, nor would I have been a particularly successful journalist. I certainly wouldn't have gone off to Africa. I'd rather pine for children than die saying to myself, 'I could have been a contender.' I *was* a contender."

Yet in the larger social picture, Gabriella concedes, "If people like me don't reproduce, civilization may be the worse for it. On both my mother and my father's side, I come from generations of academics, historians, diplomats—thinkers and doers—and as the years go by, I begin to see that far from being an exception or a maverick, I am in fact the very obvious carrier of a certain genetic inheritance. I am a typical product of my family; I can see the thread stretching back through the generations. Do I think it's a shame that this genetic inheritance won't continue? Yes, I do. I'm arrogant enough to actually think that the world will be a poorer place without my genes in it. But the fact is that I don't care enough to do anything about it. There wasn't time to do that and the other things on my list."

When I press her on the implications of a contracting European population, she readily concurs, "Many Western cities will be largely black/Hispanic/Asian in fifty years' time. Does that bother me? Well, I vaguely regret the extinction of gene lines that in their various ways played a part in the establishment of Western civilization. But the gene lines coming in from the developing world will have their own strengths, energies, and qualities, I guess." That poignant but politically charged "I guess" captures a conflicted melancholy that many liberal white Westerners will only give expression to in private—if then.

Last, I told you that Gabriella was candid, and this is the sort of statement that many a childless woman—or man, for that matter—of my generation might honestly make but that you will rarely read: "I'm an atheist. I'm a solipsist. As far as I'm concerned, while I know intellectually that the world and its inhabitants will continue after my death, it has no real meaning for me. I am terrified of and obsessed with my own extinction, and what happens next is of little interest to me. I certainly don't feel I owe the future anything, and that includes my genes and my offspring. I feel absolutely no sense of responsibility for the propagation of the human race. There are far too many human beings in the world as it is. I am happy to leave that task to someone else."

Irish-born and forty-six at the time of our interview, Nora was then an events planner for an engineering organization. She enjoyed her work, at which she was renowned for her effectiveness and good humor, but she placed equal emphasis on her life after hours. She maintains a large, lively set of friendships, and regularly partakes of the city's concerts, films, and plays. She's sharp, droll, and quick-witted.

Astonishingly, Nora and all five of her siblings have neglected to reproduce: "Each of us is quite independent, with goals that were more immediate and career-oriented than children."

Unlike Gabriella, through young adulthood Nora always assumed she would have children. Yet she is romantically fastidious and willful. Though she admits, "I went through a phase when I was coming up to thirty where I got very depressed because it appeared to me highly unlikely that I would have children," motherhood "was never so important to me as to compromise on the man." As smart, appealing women, both Nora and Gabriella might have had families were they willing to marry Mr. Not Quite Right, but kids weren't important enough. Once again, personal happiness trumps kids.

Nora is firmly resigned that children are off the table. She grants that she's "a bit" regretful, but notes, "As I grow older, I feel a greater need for solitude, and for 'me time.'

Perhaps it's work that does it—being responsible for ten staff and having a fairly 'open-door' policy makes me delight in going home, closing the door, and relishing the peace." A recent holiday to Canada with her young godson was sobering. "Yes, he's great—funny, intelligent, well mannered, interested—but I felt that the responsibility of taking him into bear country was huge. A metaphor for life, perhaps?"

Nora's maternal regrets are skin-deep. "I think I have a lovely life. I can see myself continuing to have fun, to enjoy my job, to meet interesting people, to go on great holidays, to read interesting books, to support my family and friends." (Note that I did not plant the words *fun* and *interesting* in my interviewee's mouth.) When I ask what she sees as redeeming her life, she balks. "I think that's a very Protestant question! I'm not sure my life needs redemption. Maybe I'm too much of a hedonist."

Still, Nora sorrows, "I think my parents came from an excellent gene pool, and it's a shame that to date that hasn't been passed on." Though she has many cousins, the loss of the combined heritage of her particular parents is "a sadness." As for perpetuating her ethnicity, her parents both taught Irish, and she has "a mother tongue that is under threat." But, she says, "In the wide scheme of things, I am conscious that languages disappear every year." We are of a generation grown accustomed to loss—of habitat, wilderness, biodiversity, fish. Why not Irish, too?

Be that as it may, at the end of our exchange Nora declares to me fervently, "You and I should have had children!"—hastily appending that she meant not for our own sakes, but in social terms. "We're blessed with brains, education, and good health." The longer our discourse continues, she admits, "the more I think I am a squanderer of my gifts and my heritage. But I live in a decadent age where that doesn't seem such a problem. Anyway, devoting my *whole life* to promulgating my ethnicity is a big ask."

Last, at only twenty-six, more than a generation younger than I, Leslie will have to stand in for the staggeringly numerous younger women who have shared with me their lack of enthusiasm for the familial project. When we discussed the issue, Leslie was a publicist for a small literary publishing company in London, to which she was devoted. She was very good at her job (an aptitude from which I personally benefited). Her sunny, perky quality provides a welcome counterpoint to my jaded older friends, and she's optimistic about the future; that is, hers.

Leslie does not want children. "When I think about my future, I envisage the fulfillment of ambitions such as traveling and furthering my career, not having babies. I can't imagine I will be able to give up the lifestyle I lead to become a parent. Financial independence is very important to me, as is retaining my own independence in any relationship. Something would have to give in order for me to properly care for a child, and, unfortunately, it's most often the mother who has to forgo some aspect of her life."

When I ask her, an only child, if it matters to her whether

she carries on the family line, she says honestly, "It's not really something I've thought about."

On the other hand, Leslie offers evidence that Be Here Now—living for the present—is not always morally arid. "I certainly don't see my purpose as being to perpetuate the human race. What makes my life worth living for me and also what, I think, redeems my life is my relationships and interaction with others, be they family, friends, lovers, colleagues, total strangers. I think what redeems individuals is their acts of humanity."

Moreover, like most of her generation, Leslie isn't concerned with maintaining the Anglo-Saxon identity of Britain in the slightest. "Is there any true British race now anyway? I think it's far too late to start worrying about its preservations at this stage." She has embraced multiculturalism, and faces the prospect of Western cities going majority-minority with cheer. "Most of my friends are from different ethnic backgrounds, and I feel lucky to live in London, a city full of such diverse cultures, religions, and races. I think diversity adds to British culture rather than destroys it."

As for whether she worries that she might regret giving motherhood a miss, Leslie would subject the decision to one test only: whether she might be "discontented" in the future. "But then who's to say that I would feel more content if I did have children?"

Contentment. Happiness. Satisfaction. Fun. There's nothing, strictly speaking, wrong with these concerns, but they are all of a piece. They fail to take into account that our individual lives are tiny beads in a string. Our beloved present is merely the precarious link between the past and the future—of family, ethnicity, nation, and species. We owe our very contentment—which disasters from Hurricane Katrina to Fukushima remind us relies heavily on potable water and toilets—to the ingenuity of our ancestors. Yet it rarely seems to enter the modern "childfree" head that proper payback of that debt might entail handing on the baton of our happy-happy heritage to someone else.

To the above three case studies, I would add myself. There is no generalization in this article, no matter how harsh, that would not apply to me. I care about my own life in the present. I think I should be, but—doubtless because I don't have children—I'm honestly not very fussed about what happens after I die. I'm proud of the Shriver family, but not enough to help to ensure that it outlasts me. As Nora pointed out, my genes are swell. But like my friends', my sorrow at having neglected to pass them on is vague, thin, and abstract, and no match for Be Here Now. I fancy I work very hard, but in socially crucial respects, I am lazy. Like Gabriella's, my stunted progeny are eternally eight inches high and made of pulped trees, and if they keep me up at night I can quiet them by rewriting a lousy chapter in the morning. If I feel, oh, a little wistful about the fact that the country of my birth, the United States, will probably within my lifetime no longer be peopled in majority by those of European extraction like me, that passing dismay has never been considerable enough for me to inconvenience myself by giving lifts to football practice. Frankly, if I can't be troubled to replace myself with a reasonable facsimile, immigrants willing to nurse sick little boys through their fevers have truly earned the right to take my place.

Of course, that "wistfulness" of mine is political dynamite. Yet maybe the immigration debate has sufficiently matured for us to concede that white folks are people, too. We encourage minorities of every stripe—Jamaicans, Muslims, Jews—to be proud of their heritage, as well they should be. We don't assume that if immigrants from China cherish their roots and still make a mean moo shoo pork they are therefore bigoted toward every other ethnicity on the planet. So can Italians not champion Italianness? The native British their Yorkshire pudding? White Americans their apple pie? Indeed, the tacit PC consensus—that every minority from Australian aborigines to Romanies should be treasuring, preserving, and promulgating their culture, while whites with a European heritage should not—is producing a virulent, sometimes poisonous right-wing backlash across America, Britain, and the Continent. In the interest of civil, rational thinking on this matter, we should at least allow ourselves to talk about it. Collectively, a long-dominant population is contracting, and maybe by the time we're minorities in our own countries we will have rights, too—among them, at least, the right to feel a little sad.

Meanwhile, as the West's childless have grown more prevalent, the stigma that once attached to being "barren" falls away. Women—men as well—are free to choose from a host of fascinating lives that may or may not involve children, and couples are opting for the latter in droves. My friends and I are decent people—or at least we treat each other well. We're interesting. We're *fun*. But writ large, we're an economic, cultural, and moral disaster.

There has to be something wrong when spurning reproduction doesn't make Gabriella and me the "mavericks" we'd both have prided ourselves as in our younger days but standard issue for our era. Surely the contemporary absorption with our own lives as the be-all and end-all ultimately hails from an insidious misanthropy—a lack of faith in the whole human enterprise. In its darkest form, the growing cohort of childless couples determined to throw all their money at Being Here Now—to take that step aerobics class, visit Tanzania, put an addition on the house while making no effort to ensure there's someone around to inherit the place when the party is over—has the quality of the mad, slightly hysterical scenes of gleeful abandon that fiction writers portray when imagining the end of the world.

Not to disparage old people, but *senescent* is not a pretty word. Large sectors of the Western population have broken faith with the future. In the Middle East, birthrates are still quite high, whereas many Europeans, Australians, and European Americans cannot be bothered to scrounge up another generation of even the same size—which would presumably mean fewer holidays, more tedium, less leisure time—because children might not always be interesting and fun, because they might not make us *happy*, because some days they're a pain in the butt. When Islamic fundamentalists accuse the West of being decadent, degenerate, and debauched, you have to wonder if maybe they've got a point.

THE MOST IMPORTANT THING

by

Sigrid Nunez

THERE WAS A TIME during my childhood when I believed that all children were unwanted. My own mother, a German war bride whose first child had been born out of wedlock, made no secret of the fact that having three children had not been planned, nor was it, for her, something happy making. She and my father had met at the end of World War II, when he was a soldier stationed with the occupying forces in her southern German hometown. She was eighteen years old when the first of her three daughters was born. Not until two years later, when she became pregnant again, did my parents marry (a delay that has never been explained). By the time their second daughter was born, they had moved to New York, first to the Fort Greene housing project in Brooklyn, and a few years later to another, newly built project, on Staten

Island, which would be my home from the age of two until I went off to college. The circumstances of her own youth (the war, the too-early pregnancy, the immigration to America with a husband who was in all ways an unsuitable match and whom she considered beneath her) ensured that she would always see herself as unlucky, as someone who had been cheated. Whatever good might come her way from having had a family (and that good would not come before the children were grown), it was the bad that marked her, that made her life what it was.

Part of it—a very large part, surely—was that, like her own mother, she was not a maternal woman. To her, a child, any child, was a brat.

Speaking about one of the neighbors, she would say, "She's pregnant again," rolling her eyes in contempt. About someone she'd run into at the mall: "Her stomach is out to *there*." As if this were some kind of disgrace. To hear my mother, you would never think expecting a baby could mean anything good, let alone *a bundle of joy*.

But she was not one of a kind. When I think of the people among whom I grew up, it's as if I were looking back not fifty but more than a hundred years, to an era before modern beliefs in the sacredness of childhood and children's rights had emerged, before childhood had come to be seen as a time of innocence deserving protection, the part of every person's life that should be carefree and full of fun.

I am talking about people whose lives were harder than

most, people with low-paying jobs or dependent on welfare, people with limited education, foreign accents, poor English, bad teeth, dark skin—people who were all too aware of being at the bottom of the ladder. Their inevitable frustrations were, inevitably, taken out at home. Husbands beat wives; parents beat children; big children beat little children. (Don't let's think about the pets.) And just because a child was too young to earn a living didn't mean he or she couldn't be put to work. I remember children who spent far more hours doing housework and other chores than at play. In some families, unlike our own, it was understood that such chores took priority over reading, schoolwork, or any kind of study.

Though I can recall many who were good-hearted, I can think of few women in our neighborhood who'd bring to mind the word *maternal*. The dominant emotion toward children, from mothers and fathers both, seemed to be anger. It was part of the chaos of that place and time: you never knew when some grown-up was going to fly off the handle. Children were forever being screamed at, sworn at, slapped around, or worse. (*Goddamn kids*: heard so often we could have been forgiven for thinking that if the Pied Piper of Hamelin had come to town, our parents would not have wept.) The berating or whipping of a child in public, often before a smirking crowd, was nothing rare. And the suffering of anyone subjected to that particular humiliation was so obvious and so dreadful that it was hard to believe the parent inflicting it could possibly also love that child. One girl

I knew was so devastated by the experience that she later jumped out a window (thankfully, one low enough that she survived).

My mother was not alone in her habit of attributing almost all errancy on the part of children to malice rather than to carelessness or weakness or ignorance. Children were manipulative; they were *little con artists*, masters of sophisticated cunning. Outpourings of childish emotion were often dismissed as faking, or *just a bid for attention*. Even getting sick was viewed with suspicion: *You could have made it to the bathroom!* In elementary school, many of the teachers also appeared to be stuck in a darker age when children—boys, especially—were seen as nasty by nature, short adults who, unless relentlessly shamed and disciplined, above all corporally (usually by paddling, but I can recall countless episodes of more serious roughing up), were sure to grow up rotten. (The existence of ample proof in that increasingly crime-ridden community that this kind of punishment was having the exact opposite effect of deterrence went ignored.)

At some point, of course, I came to understand that not all children had been unwanted, and that, like people everywhere, most of the parents I knew, the mothers in particular, had counted having a family among their life's sweetest dreams. The problem for many of them arose from being unable to prevent having *more* children than they'd wanted, or from having them come along at times when they couldn't help being more burden—*Another mouth to feed! Where's he gonna sleep?*—than blessing. And I began to understand how a person could love his or her children and at the same time deeply resent them. *I didn't ask to be born!* How familiar is the defensive child's self-pitying cry. But I have known many whose lives were formed—or deformed, perhaps I should say—by having been made to feel guilty for all the trouble they caused by coming into the world.

Yet none of this meant that I didn't want to have children myself. More accurately, I took it for granted that I would. Motherhood was like school; it was inescapable. It went along with marriage—and I didn't know any girl who imagined a future for herself that didn't include marriage. It's true that you could always point to one or two women about whom it was said, "She never married; she was a career girl." But such women were never held up as models, and if there was something about being a secretary or a teacher or a nurse (pretty much the only careers open to women back then) that was more wonderful than being a wife and mother, it was hard to see what it was. (The oddball female who was content to be married without having kids was invariably described as being too selfish for motherhood, an occupation seen as demanding such great self-sacrifice that it was second only to taking the veil.)

And besides, I liked babies. There was one in particular, the youngest child of the family that lived next door, with whom I was even obsessed. I remember thinking little David was the most beautiful thing I'd ever seen. Whenever he appeared I would stop whatever I was doing to stare at him, wondering equally at his Gerber-baby perfection and at the tumult of wrenching tenderness within. Love. I was eight years old. His mother indulged my plea for a photograph, which became a prized possession. In school I made him the subject of a writing assignment, not a word of which I can remember today. But I never forgot the response—from my teacher and from the principal, to whom she showed it, and from my mother and from David's mother, to whom my mother showed it. This might have been the first time I understood that if you cared passionately about something and you managed to express it by putting down certain words in a certain order, you could touch people; you could win their praise.

And I would always love children. In fact, I find those who do not strange and even frightening. I get flustered when a person says to me, "I don't like children." *I was a child,* I want to say.

Once, when I was six or seven, walking with my mother down a certain mean Brooklyn street, we passed a group of surly-looking boys gathered on a stoop. As my mother quickened her steps, dragging me along, one of the boys threw something at me: the wooden stick from an ice-cream pop he'd just finished eating. I tugged my mother's hand. "Mommy, that boy hit me!" Marching on, staring grimly ahead, she addressed me in a voice that was like a slap: "And what do you think I can do about it?" At which a certain knowledge sank into my bones, and with that knowledge a fear that would never wholly leave me.

In Book Three of his autobiographical novel, *My Strug-*

gle, the Norwegian writer Karl Ove Knausgaard writes about the terror his father made him feel—"every single day of my entire childhood"—and how he would console himself with fantasies of dying. About raising his own children, Knausgaard says, "I have tried to achieve only one aim: that they shouldn't be afraid of their father."

I remember that when the time came to think seriously about whether or not to have children, the same idea occurred to me: the crucial thing would be to make sure that they not be afraid of their mother. It was a goal I believed I could achieve. But there was something else. As a child, I never felt safe. *Every single day of my entire childhood* I lived in fear that something bad was going to happen to me. I live like that still. And so the big question: How could a person who lived like that ever make a child feel safe?

The more I thought about it, the more convinced I became that there was nothing harder to accomplish in life than being a good parent. The store of patience and wisdom and kindness that seemed to be required was truly daunting; I wasn't sure that I myself possessed even the minimum to prevent catastrophe. But when I looked around, from what I could tell, this could have been said of a lot of people.

It was not that I thought most people were bound to make *terrible* parents, only that the group that would make ideal parents was surprisingly small—especially given that those who chose to have children far outnumbered those who did not.

I remember a woman, a mentor, who once asked me if I

thought I'd make a good mother. When I told her honestly that I didn't know, she was mightily displeased. It was as if I'd confessed to being a bad person. But I am astonished at those who are unfazed by the prospect of child raising. A male friend of mine, childless but confident, once assured me, "You just give them lots and lots of love." Perhaps only a man could believe it is as simple as that.

I belong to that generation of American and European women who, having come of age in the 1960s, discovered that so great a gap existed between our mothers and ourselves that we had almost nothing in common. And for us, the lucky daughters, reliable birth control, legal abortion, and changes in attitudes toward a woman's rights and her place in society brought about possibilities the likes of which women before us could only dream. *She never married; she was a career girl* (like *I see you girls are all alone tonight*) was now something to laugh at, a line from some scathing feminist joke.

If I had grown up shaky about the kind of parent I'd make, I believed from early on that I had a vocation to be a writer. Although in my youthful, naive way I gravely underestimated how difficult such a life would be, I stuck to it, and I was steadfast in not letting other things distract me.

No young woman aspiring to a literary career could ignore the fact that the women writers of highest achievement, women like Jane Austen, the Brontës, George Eliot, and Virginia Woolf, did not have children. Colette, who wrote beautifully and piercingly about her own mother, gave birth to an unwanted daughter whom she neglected. Doris Lessing declared herself "not the best person" to raise the two young children she left behind when she moved from southern Africa to London to pursue her career. Why? "There is nothing more boring for an intelligent woman than to spend endless amounts of time with small children."

Another fact hard to ignore: motherhood is one of the most significant as well as one of the most widely shared of all human experiences. In Western culture, it has always been essentially synonymous with womanhood. Yet who can name a major novel by a canonical writer, male or female, that takes motherhood for its main subject?

If you were a girl who loved above all to read and write and who could not imagine an adulthood in which these activities did not hold a central place, you probably knew even before puberty that you were headed for conflict. For is it not a truth universally acknowledged that, for a woman, the central place is reserved for her kids?

"And then my children were born," writes Natalia Ginzburg, in an essay called "My Vocation," "and when they were very little I could not understand how anyone could sit herself down to write if she had children. I began to feel contempt for my vocation. Now and again I longed for it desperately and felt that I was in exile, but I tried to despise it and make fun of it. I spent my time wondering whether there was sun or not or wind or not so that I could take the children out for a walk."

There must be thousands of gifted, ambitious women who have been haunted by the case of Sylvia Plath, perhaps none so much as those who came of age around the time of her transformation from a gifted, ambitious, and tragically self-destructive woman into a celebrity feminist myth. The American edition of *The Bell Jar*, Plath's only novel, appeared in 1971, eight years after its (pseudonymous) publication in England, where, a month later, at the age of thirty, Plath had killed herself. From that highly autobiographical book and from her many confessional poems, as well as from a collection of letters to her family that was published in 1975, and from the reminiscences by various people that came out in the wake of her death, a horrible-fascinating story emerged.

Here was a woman who could not have been more sensitive to the competing demands of career and family, a woman who appears never to have been without an anguished ambivalence toward motherhood, about which she wrote brilliantly and sometimes hysterically, morbidly. Though genius and pathology set Plath well apart from most other literary aspirants, as from most people in general, it was, for many women, an irresistible temptation to read lessons into that doomed life. That she had wanted to have it all was indisputable. ("I am the girl who wants to be God," she told her diary.) Fierce ambition was there from the start, the determination to "whip" herself "onward and upward." Always, the desire to write great things, not merely to succeed but to be famous, immortal. But the rest of life must not be left out. The promising poet must also marry (and the man, it goes without saying, must be someone even smarter and more talented than she) and start making babies while still a dewy young thing. And in all matters having to do with the role of wife and mother, such as cooking and housekeeping, she must also shine. Plath could not bear the thought that her intelligence and ambition might take away from her womanliness. On the other hand, even as a schoolgirl she had worried about future motherhood holding her back from literary achievement, which, for her, meant not just sitting down to write, but being prolific, winning prizes, publishing a best seller.

Like Ginzburg, she would make room for thinking about whether the sun or wind was right for taking the children out for a walk. But to feel contempt for her vocation, to despise or make fun of it, was unthinkable. And she would not be "exiled." Rather than take time off from work as Ginzburg did, and as so many other mothers of young children do, she would go full speed in the other direction. Writer, supermom, domestic goddess—why couldn't a woman be all three? *Live to the hilt! To the top!* The motto of her fellow poet Anne Sexton, who also suffered from mental illness and also took her own life, could have been Plath's own.

What she seemed not yet to have learned was that it is one thing—and an extremely good thing—to be a perfectionist writer but quite another to be a perfectionist wife and mother because, in the latter case, too much lies outside one's control.

If she hadn't given up her first two children, said Lessing—who believed this act of hers had been brave—if instead she'd been forced to spend all her time with them, she would have ended up an alcoholic. I am surely not alone in wondering how different Sylvia Plath's life might have been if she hadn't chosen to start a family at the same time that she was trying to launch her career. I had a college professor who, with Plath's story very much in mind, used to warn her female creative writing students: "You girls all want to set up your domestic lives before your careers, and that's a mistake."

It is soothing, then, to consider Virginia Woolf, who, though she, too, suffered from depression and psychotic breaks, and ended up, aged fifty-nine, in the River Ouse, was capable of a kind of contentment and fulfillment that Plath in her much-shorter life never found. Woolf might be called angry, for she was that, and she might be called bitchy, for at times she was that, too. But she was not cruel like Plath. She was not filled with hatred like Plath. She was not as calculating or vengeful or paranoid as Plath, and she does not seem to have been as deranged. Taken as a whole, and despite its grim ending, Woolf's life strikes us as one of enviable beauty and dignity, full of soaring triumphs and humble, everyday satisfactions. (Having a stable marriage, as Plath did not, was surely a big help.)

Yet Woolf, too, fretted about the kind of woman she was and sometimes beat herself up for being inadequate. A history of mental disorder had led doctors to advise her strongly against having children—advice with which neither she nor her husband quarreled. But still there came a day when she looked back and thought that, in spite of all she had achieved as a writer, not having children meant that her life had been a failure.

I believe that fear of being a failure plays a large part in goading many women who are ambivalent about motherhood into maternity.

That, and the fear of missing out, as neatly put by the narrator of this one-sentence story by Lydia Davis called "A Double Negative":

> *At a certain point in her life, she realizes it is not so much that she wants to have a child as that she does not want not to have a child, or not to have had a child.*

There is no ignoring society's expectation that its members shall reproduce. ("Happy Mother's Day," a barista automatically greets me, even though I am by myself.) Resisters must be prepared for widespread disapproval and even, in some communities, isolation. Object of curiosity, pity, embarrassment, scorn: I am keenly aware of having been, at one time or another, all of these—though, in my case, I'd say this has had as much to do with my remaining single as with my being childless.

Any person who marries but rejects procreation is seen as unnatural. But a woman who confesses never to have felt the desire for a baby is considered a freak. Women have always been raised to believe they would not be complete and could not be thought to have succeeded in life without the experience of motherhood. (Did Woolf believe that her husband's life must also be judged a failure for reasons of childlessness? I doubt it.) That there could be something in the world that a woman could want more than children has been viewed as unacceptable. Things may be marginally different now, but, even if there is something she wants more than children, that is no reason for a woman to remain childless. Any normal woman, it is understood, wants—and should want—both.

A graduate student of mine tells me, with some heat, "I do plan to have kids one day, but I certainly hope they won't be the most important thing in my life!"

Am I wrong to think that perhaps, if this is how she feels and continues to feel, she ought at least to consider not having kids?

I can hear her respond, with equal heat, "But that's not fair. You wouldn't say that to a man."

In any case, she will learn soon enough that her honesty isn't likely to be met with understanding. When Michelle Obama (to name just one prominent, accomplished woman) announces, "I'm a mother *first*," she is of course saying what most people want to hear. (It is inconceivable that any woman running for public office today could get away with explaining that although she loves her children dearly, for her, being a leader comes first. President Obama has often been heard to say, meaningfully, "I am a father." No one leans in expecting to hear *first*.)

Grace Paley once jeered at the idea that had been put over on women that taking care of children was a profession, a specialization, that had to be done perfectly. To her, this reeked of self-importance. "That is not a profession for grown-up people, to bring up one child," she said. "It's a joke."

Jeanette Winterson has said she does not believe her own literary success would have been possible if she had been heterosexual. In an interview she gave to *The Paris Review* in 1997, she said, "I can't find a model, a female literary model who did the work she wanted to do and led an ordinary heterosexual life and had children. Where is she?" Speaking of her younger self, Winterson said, "There was a part of me that instinctively knew that in order to be able to pursue my life, which was going to be hard enough anyway, I would be much better off either on my own or with a woman."

Things have changed since 1997. It is no longer only heterosexual couples who create nuclear families. Still, I imagine countless women nodding when they read on: "The issue of how women are going to live with men and bring up children and perhaps do the work they want to do has in no way been honestly addressed."

These days you might say the issue has, in fact, been honestly addressed, though without bringing it any closer to being honestly resolved.

Winterson was born in 1959. In the interview, she mentions how for some women of her generation, the solution was thought to be putting off maternity until they were near middle age—more or less my old professor's advice not to set up your domestic life ahead of your career. What happened to them, Winterson says, was that they ended up exhausted.

A generation later, at least among people I know (mostly other writers, artists, and academics), many more men are involved with child care, and to a far greater extent, than used to be the case. Nevertheless, as we keep getting told—as if we needed to be told—in most American households, the burden of what has always been thought of as woman's work (known for damn good reason as never done), including the child care, still falls to the woman, whether or not she also works outside the home, whether or not she outearns her husband, whether or not she has, or is trying to have, a career. In fact, there are plenty of working mothers who do 100 percent of the housework. And for every writer father I know whose career is if not thriving, at least progressing, I know a writer mother whose career is stuck or in decline and who is struggling to get by as much as any woman I've ever known. Speaking of struggling, I want to add that although women have always written fiction about the experience of taking care of children, it is only with Knausgaard's *Struggle*, an international literary hit that contains much minutely detailed description of such things as diaper changing, baby feeding, and dealing with tantrums, that the world has sat up and found this confessional domestic material, now that it is revealed through male eyes, not just worthy of interest but sensational.

Three years before Winterson, Alice Munro also gave an interview to *The Paris Review*, in which she said: "I think I married to be able to write, to settle down and give my attention back to the important thing. Sometimes now when

I look back at those early years I think, 'This was a hard-hearted young woman.'" Munro confesses to not having been there for her small children and knowing that they suffered for it. "When my oldest daughter was about two, she'd come to where I was sitting at the typewriter, and I would bat her away with one hand and type with the other. . . . This was bad because it made her the adversary to what was most important to me."

Back to the important thing. What was most important to me. Make no mistake, this was a writer first. More recently, in an interview for *The New Yorker*, answering a question about whether she considers herself a feminist writer (she does not), Munro says, "I do think it's plenty hard to be a man. Think if I'd had to support a family, in those early years of failure?"

Here's my question: Is there any way for a woman in the young Munro's position to escape being judged—by herself, by the world—as hard-hearted?

All the years when I was considering whether to have a child, I kept wondering how on earth this was supposed to work. It did not help that among older, established writers I knew, there were precious few models. What I saw was a huge group of dysfunctional (mostly divorced) parents whose children all seemed to have problems. It did not help that with each passing childbearing year, I was discovering more and more how incompatible my writing life was with any other kind of life. For one thing, writing turned out to be a torturous process. (I might not have been able to relate directly, but when David Rakoff described writing as being like having his teeth pulled out—through his penis—I thought that I couldn't have said it better myself.) For another thing, I wanted to write novels, and there was no getting around the fact that novel writing required long stretches of uninterrupted solitude. Many times, just having a man in my life seemed like one person too many, with the relationship inevitably coming between me and my work. And since writing novels is rarely a lucrative profession, like almost all writers, I had to do some other kind of work in order to live, meaning that a substantial amount of time had to be given up to teaching. Finally, it did not help that my career coincided with a period in which the publishing industry has been in a state of chronic instability, not to say crisis, forcing me and most writers I know to accept precariousness and unrelenting anxiety as occupational hazards. All this contributed to my sense that starting a family was as reasonable as building a house on quicksand.

Who knows. If I'd gone ahead and had a child, maybe what happened to Natalia Ginzburg would also have happened to me. I would have begun to feel contempt for writing, my bundle of joy replacing it as the most important thing. This is not impossible for me to imagine. But the picture that comes far more readily to mind is one in which I am typing with one hand and batting a toddler away with the other. And how would I have felt in that situation? I know exactly how I would have felt: angry, frustrated, burning with resentment toward the child, and no doubt toward its father, too. Full of self-loathing, tormented with guilt for having made my child the adversary to my vocation. And if there is one thing I am certain would have destroyed me, it is this conflict.

Because, in the end, it came down to another question I kept asking myself: Can I be the kind of mother I would have wanted to have? *Just give them lots and lots of love*—oh, this I believed I could do. But I also believed that writing had saved my life and that if I could not write, I would die. And so long as this was true, and so long as writing continued to be the enormously difficult thing it has always been for me, I didn't think I could be a real mother. Not the kind I would have wanted for my child. The kind to whom he or she was the most important thing, object of that unconditional love for which I had desperately yearned as a child myself and the want of which I have never gotten over. "Children detect things like that," acknowledged Munro.

Some years ago, my mother, a big animal lover, was devastated by the death of her dog. "You know," she confessed to me, "I feel worse than I would if you had died." This is somewhat less awful than it sounds. At the time, she and I had been estranged for years, whereas she and the dog had been companions for almost as long and now its death had left her alone. In fact, even before she said it, imagining how bereft she must feel, I'd had the same thought myself.

My mother was not without kindness or decency. She did not abandon her children or neglect them. But she could not forgive us our existence. (*I didn't ask to be born!*) She was human, and we humans always insist that someone must pay for life's unfairness to us. If nothing else had made me a feminist, this would have been enough: the fate of women like her, forced by society to give their lives to something they neither wanted nor were in any way suited for. Of her three daughters, none would give birth. One decided to adopt; it did not go well.

Mother. "The holiest thing alive," according to English Romantic poet and philosopher Samuel Taylor Coleridge. Our own culture likes to sentimentalize motherhood with a certain kind of mushy tribute, as in those Procter & Gamble "Thank you, Mom" commercials aired during the Olympics. But if being a mom really were something held in high esteem—if it were even regarded with the same respect as other work that people do—women everywhere would probably be a lot happier and more fulfilled than we know them to be.

Now that I have passed the age Woolf was when she died, I can look back and say, thank God, I do not feel that my life has been a failure because I didn't have children. (A failure in other ways, yes, for other reasons, but not for that one.) To forgo motherhood was the right thing to do. But whether it was a choice I made or one that was made for me is perhaps another question.

"But you love children," people say to me. Meaning, surely I must have regrets. It is true that I'd rather spend an afternoon hanging out with someone's kids than with many adults I know. And not too much time passes in the course of my days without my remembering that I have missed one of life's most significant experiences. But let me say this: the idea of having it all has always been foreign to me. I grew up believing that if you worked incredibly hard *and* were incredibly lucky, you might get to have *one* dream in life come true. Going for everything was a dangerous, distracting fantasy. I believe I have been incredibly lucky.

MOMMY FEAREST

by

Anna Holmes

I SPENT THE ENTIRE ninth year of my life horrified that I was pregnant. It began at the tail end of second grade, and continued on until I was ten, when my mom innocently handed me a book that explained the particulars of human development and made perfectly clear that pregnancy could not come before menarche. At the time, I was living with my parents and my little sister on the northern edge of a California college town, where, after school, the neighbor kids and I played on the dark gray macadam of our quiet cul-de-sac, and sometimes, in and around the drainage pond at the end of the street, some two hundred yards away. There were tiny fish in that pond, and nearby, crows, and gophers, and probably a fair number of snakes, although I saw evidence of the latter only once, when I rode my bike past the corpse of an unlucky garter, his skull flattened by the thick tread of one of the motorized bikes that pimply teenage boys rode, whizzing up and over the packed hills of dirt on the farthest reaches of the pond.

The "pond," as we called it, was nothing more than a place where runoff was collected, and, one assumes, drained, but it was teeming with life: cattails, dragonflies, mosquitoes, tadpoles, and, later in the season, baby frogs. I played there by myself, and sometimes with my friend Rachel, and sometimes with Daniel, a boy two years my junior who lived in a duplex three doors down from my family's one-story Streng Brothers–designed home. Daniel was shorter than I was, covered in freckles, and probably Scottish in descent—he shared a surname with the man who later became my husband and then ex-husband—and his straight hair stuck out at odd angles, like the bristles on a stiff brush. He was not blessed with a particularly compelling personality—the most interesting thing about him was the fact that he had accidentally aided in the strangulation of his family's pet cat after he left a string around her neck that got snagged on the slat of a wooden fence—but he was the only boy on the block, which meant that he could be counted on to do the things other kids my age didn't want to do, like racing our bikes around, and playing Cyclops, and covering ourselves in the Capay soils native to our area as we brandished plastic shovels and tried to dig our way to China.

Daniel could also be counted on, at least for a few months, to drop trou and show me his penis. I wouldn't call what we did "playing doctor," because I had no interest in the medical arts or in feigning illness in order to get a glimpse of someone else's forbidden flesh. Despite my straightforwardness about what we did, however, I was well aware that there was perhaps something tawdry about pulling down my drawers to expose my genitals to a neighbor boy—and, even worse, asking him to do the same—but I didn't care: I wanted to get a gander at the goods. Some days, we'd meet up after school and squeeze into the narrow space next to the eastern wall of my house, pull down our pants on the count of three, and spend a few minutes eyeballing one another. Eventually, looking begat discussing, which begat touching, which begat the one day in the summer of 1981, after capturing four baby frogs and placing them in a Mason jar for safekeeping, I pulled down my pants, had Daniel do the same, and thrust myself up against him. We stood there for ten seconds or so, my knees bent and my hips tilted upward so I could snuggle his little penis between my legs more easily—I was a good five inches taller than he was—but soon he got nervous, wiggled back into his shorts, and set out for home. The next morning, after discovering that the baby frogs we'd captured had perished in the suffocating conditions of the sealed glass jar, it occurred to me that the previous day's sexual child's play might have made me pregnant, and I spent the next year in a state of mild panic, examining, whenever I remembered to do so, my bare belly for the swelling that suggested evidence of human gestation. None ever came.

I did get pregnant later. I was nineteen, and in love, and

having the sort of constant, frenzied, and, yes, unprotected sex that many of those in the midst of early adulthood know not to engage in but engage in anyway. (I would become pregnant twice more, once when I was twenty-four, and again when I was twenty-seven.) The first termination took place at a Planned Parenthood in downtown Sacramento, California, and I was terrified but resolute: there had never been any doubt in my mind as to whether I would go through with the pregnancy, and little concern as to whether I might later regret the removal of the mass of cells embedded in the walls of my uterus. I didn't, and I didn't regret the next abortion, or the next one, although I did marvel, in later years, at the fact that had I taken these pregnancies to term, I would, at thirty-five years of age, be a mother to, respectively, a sixteen-year-old, a ten-year-old, and an eight-year-old. I found the idea amusing—and utterly, completely terrifying.

That terror, that utter horror, had very little to do with my feelings about children and everything to do with my feelings about myself, namely, my hunger to do things, and meet people, and carve out a special space in the world in which I could find my authentic self, whatever that came to mean. Motherhood had never been of particular fascination for me—my one and only youthful foray into performative parenting involved a Baby Wet & Care, a doll manufactured by Kenner that was designed to break out in a diaper rash after being "fed" a bottle of water and wetting a diaper. In fact, from the time I was a young girl until well into my thirties,

I did not fantasize about having babies, or find others' babies of much, if any, interest. (My own baby sister, born when I was four, was met, I am told, with a warmth and affection one notch below my reverence for things like *Sesame Street* and illustrated children's encyclopedias. But maybe that's the way it is for every kid with a new sibling. Regardless, I love her very much.)

Part of this was, no doubt, a function of the era—the 1980s—in which I was raised, a time when the birthrate of the United States was in the midst of a lull that had begun back in the mid-'70s economic recession. And though the country's conservatism was reflected, to some degree, in its popular culture, which still relied on depictions of functional, conventional, nuclear families in order to sell time to advertisers, the female heads of households in those narratives—Clair Huxtable on *The Cosby Show*, Elyse Keaton on *Family Ties*, the eponymous heroines of *Kate & Allie*, to name some television examples—were more than just moms: they were also, for the most part, career women. (Allie stayed home and took care of housekeeping and the kids until the show's fifth season, when she and Kate started a catering service.) As such, their fealty to their kids was profound but not prohibitive: one got the sense that they did not locate their successes, and certainly not their senses of self, within the comings and goings of the minors under their care. In fact, sometimes children of '80s-era television women were so ancillary to their mothers' identities as to be almost beside the point: after the high-powered Murphy Brown decided to go it alone and give birth to a baby she would raise as a single mom, her son all but disappeared from the series writers' radar.

Mothers who are able to successfully combine work and family are all around me, yet the compatibility of career and kids remains a concept I understand intellectually but seem emotionally unable to accept. And so when I tell people—usually female friends—that, at age forty-one, I "don't know" if I want children or still feel that I'm "not ready," what I'm really saying is that I don't believe I can do the things I want to do in life and also be a parent to kids, nor am I willing to find out. Fueling this tension is a deep and paralyzing fear, a fear that, again, is not so much about children but about my own latent caretaking instincts. I suspect I would be a good mother—a fantastic mother, even—thanks to the gifts bestowed upon me by my own parents: the ability to give and express love, the indulgence of curiosity, and the prioritizing of imagination, education, and personal integrity over societally approved successes like financial or social achievement. (I take an inordinate amount of pride in my own emotional intelligence, but that particular gift has little to do with my parents and almost everything to do with the tens of thousands of dollars I've spent on psychotherapy over the past twenty years.) But herein lies the rub: as it stands now, I suspect that my commitment to and delight in parenting would be so formidable that it would take precedence over anything and everything else in my life; that my mastery of motherhood would eclipse my need for—or ability to achieve—success in any other arena. Basically, I'm afraid of my own competence.

My therapist would describe this as magical thinking—and she might be right. But the example set by my own mother is one that informs much about my decision to not have kids, and her story fills me with both pride and guilt. A skinny, curious Midwestern girl who escaped her insular, tiny Ohio town and headed east to New York City, where she earned the first of two graduate degrees, worked in social justice, and traveled the world, my mother found herself, a decade and a half later, trapped in a wholly unremarkable suburb ten miles west of Sacramento, California, teaching typing skills to snotty thirteen-year-olds and supporting two grumpy daughters desperate to be left alone in their rooms except for occasional shopping trips to Macy's in search of Guess? jeans.

Is this the life she imagined for herself? My mother would no doubt take issue with what I've just written. She would flinch at the idea that her two children are anything but beautiful blessings, beings made from love between her and my adoring father, conduits through which she was able to channel all of her love, and to experience and further indulge her curiosity and wonder at the world. (Not to mention her politics.) She would deny that she lost something of herself in motherhood, and, though she might concede to having felt the occasional bout of frustration, and maybe even acknowledge a relationship between child rearing and ambitions left

unfulfilled, she would maintain that she had never commu-
nicated this to her children with any specificity. She'd be
right; she did not. But my sister and I did not need to hear
our mother acknowledge how much parenting—much of it
single parenting—limited her life; we saw it every day. We
understood that by devoting her life to us, she was, in some
ways, giving up herself. (As for my dad, well, let's be clear:
this neglect of self in the service of children, while not wholly
specific to women, is at the very least highly specific to them.
Women have long been responsible for a disproportionate
amount of the child care.)

Some might call my trepidation at the idea of motherhood
"selfishness"—I would call it "agency"—but those people are
probably either (1) dudes or (2) self-satisfied professional parents, and I'm not sure I care enough about their opinions that
I wouldn't just agree with them and shrug my shoulders in
shared chagrin. (Those who inquire after my plans for parenthood often interpret my childlessness as a function of my
dislike for kids, when, again, nothing could be further from
the truth: the barrenness of my womb has nothing to do with
a distaste for kids, who, along with animals, I like and iden-
tify with more than I do with most adults.) But the fact is,
it is never far from my mind that the means of reproduction—
and its costs—are beasts of burden borne, historically, by the
fairer sex.

Times have changed, of course, and men are shoulder-
ing more of the responsibilities of parenting—and tethering
themselves to the Snuglis and BabyBjörns—but the demands

on and expectations of women, at least in the highly educated and relatively affluent milieu I inhabit, have not so much disappeared as shifted to other things, namely, a set of insidious though by no means unprecedented expectations for the maintenance of outward appearances. (The term *MILF*, which, for the uninitiated, is an acronym for the phrase "Mother I'd Like to Fuck," only gained widespread popularity some fifteen years ago.)

Nowhere are these hoary ideas about womanhood—this performance of perfect femininity—more routinely on display than on the streets of the South Brooklyn neighborhood that I inhabit, which is lined with low-cal frozen yogurt shops and yoga and Pilates studios and overpriced boutiques filled with one-of-a-kind maternity clothes and hundred-dollar sets of receiving blankets made of "all organic cotton." One recent Mother's Day, on my way to meet two friends for an early dinner of pizza and beer, I walked by an apparel shop displaying a sandwich board exhorting (presumably unintentionally childless) female passersby who felt sad about the holiday to come in and buy a dress that would get them "knocked up in no time." Add to that the creeping commodification of childhood in the form of must-have status symbols—baby carriages, sleeper clothing—and the economic inequalities and educational failures that find parents signing up their toddlers for placement in private elementary schools years in advance and you've got yet another reason for some of the aversion I have for the demands of modern American parenthood.

In the end, maybe my ambivalence about motherhood comes down to the fact that I just don't trust myself enough. (Or that I need to move somewhere far, far away from New York, where kids can play safely in the dirt, and grocery store aisles are blessedly free of four-dollar single-serve pouches of sweet-potato-and-pear puree made from organic vegetables gathered by exoticized indigenous populations living south of the U.S. border.) But I believe that there is something else going on here, a societal discomfort not just with women who choose to remain childless but with those who decide to become mothers and dare to confess to feelings of frustration and exasperation over the choices they have made. In the spring of 2014, just five months after becoming the first lady of New York City, Chirlane McCray was excoriated by the city's tabloid newspapers for having the gall to suggest in an interview that the arrival of her first child, Chiara, was celebrated with anything but complete and utter devotion. "I was forty years old; I had a life," Ms. McCray told *New York* magazine. "But the truth is, I could not spend every day with her. I didn't want to do that. I looked for all kinds of reasons not to do it . . . I've been working since I was fourteen, and that part of me is me. It took a long time for me to get into 'I'm taking care of kids,' and what that means." (The editors of *The New York Post* interpreted these comments to mean that Ms. McCray was a "bad mom" and said as much, in huge type, on the cover of their paper's May 19 edition.)

———

What McCray left unsaid, but what I suspect she was also getting at, is that it often takes a long time for women to "get into" taking care of *themselves*, and that her need for autonomy was as much about basking in her hard-won self-actualization as it was a reaction to the exhaustion that comes with tending to a child's every need. These days, as I enter my forties, I find that I am only now beginning to feel comfortable in my own skin, to find the wherewithal to respect my own needs as much as others', to know what my emotional and physical limits are, and to confidently, yet kindly, tell others no. (No, I cannot perform that job; no, I cannot meet you for coffee; no, I cannot be in a relationship in which I feel starved for emotional and physical connection.) Despite (or because of) my single status right now, becoming a mother would feel like a devolution as much as an evolution, and the irony is that if and when I reach the point where I feel able to give my all to another human being and still keep some semblance of the self I've worked so hard to create, I will probably not be of childbearing age. Them's the breaks.

AMATEURS

by

Michelle Huneven

I WENT TO a fortune-teller when I was twenty-five. Her house was on a busy street, its shingled siding painted a strange marigold orange, the trim a clashing bright red and blue. A banner advertised, "Special: $5."

The fortune-teller, a pale, sharp-eyed woman in her forties with wild crow-black hair, ran her operation in a dark front room crowded with furniture. Lamp shades were draped with red and purple scarves. A milky cantaloupe-size crystal ball rested on a stand in the middle of a round oak table, but the fortune-teller made no move toward it—clearly the befogged ball was not for bargain shoppers. She had me sit at the table beside her, and she took my right hand. Turning my wrist, smoothing back my fingers, she studied my palm.

"You might as well get used to being poor," she said. "Money is coming, but it's a long way off."

Also, she said, I would contend with a disease, serious but not necessarily life-threatening.

And I would have one child.

I wondered then and afterward about the fortune-teller's cosmic source: When did that font of future knowledge believe that life began? At conception? Or upon the first intake of breath? Had my one chance at motherhood already come and gone?

I had broken up with my last boyfriend some months before. An agoraphobic actor who lived week to week in a flea-bag hotel, he'd already faded from my thoughts. So I was stunned when, during a routine pelvic exam, the doctor palpated my uterus and announced that I was pregnant. Quite pregnant, actually. Close to three months pregnant, the doctor said, which meant that a regrettable instance of breakup sex had caused this. If I wanted to terminate the pregnancy without going into labor, the doctor went on, I should do so within the next few days. I made an appointment for Monday and took the weekend to think it over.

I was living in Pasadena in a funky apartment complex filled with old high school friends. When I left the doctor's office, that's where I went.

My best friend said, "Don't get an abortion—you'll wreck your karma!"

I worried about my karma, but I had no partner (and I certainly couldn't be tied to the last one) and no money. I was working part-time in a coffee shop while trying to write. Our lovely low-rent apartment complex didn't allow children. And even if it had, and even if I had been flush and happily mated, I didn't feel ready or remotely capable of raising a child. Children seemed as far off as false teeth, and interested me about as much. In fact, kids aroused my impatience and jealousy, especially when their parents fussed over them or, worse, stopped everything to reason with them. I'd grown up without that kind of attention, and I begrudged it to others, even babies.

That Monday, I wrecked my karma.

It was a few weeks after that when I sat with the fortune-teller, palm upturned, and wondered if I still had one child in my future, or if, along with my karma, I'd blown my one chance. I was in no hurry to find out. If motherhood was in the cards, it was still far, far off.

First comes love. And love is what I craved. A great, trans-formational love. Love that would fill the nauseating pitch-black void lodged somewhere behind my sternum.

My late twenties and early thirties were spent in a series of time-consuming, life-swallowing love affairs. A great deal of drinking was also involved. I'd discovered alcohol's mag-ical properties in high school: here, at last, was a way to feel at home in the world. Alcohol instantly removed my psychic pain. I drank daily (but not, initially, to excess) from age eigh-teen on.

Meanwhile, my friends got married. They married each other, or friends of friends, or someone they met at work or at a party. Nobody was making the great love match of the century. Nor was anybody in a great hurry to have children. Birth control had been a big game changer in that regard; we boomers could put off having children. And we all did.

But then, in our thirties, a shift. By the late eighties, babies began to arrive.

One friend said that buying a house made her want to fill the rooms.

Another friend was so in love with her much-older husband, she had to have his babies.

Two friends had difficulty conceiving. After years of frustration and heartbreak, they both tried IVF; one couple produced a baby, the other couple ended up adopting the daughter of a fifteen-year-old from Bakersfield.

Still-single friends longing for children lowered their standards for mates; one took on the town drunk, rehabilitating him long enough for him to marry and impregnate her.

Another friend, at forty-one, seduced a twenty-year-old box boy at the local supermarket, and raised their beautiful son as a single mom.

I waited to feel what my friends did. Or an inkling thereof.

I attended the baby showers and loathed the fussy luncheons, the cringeworthy games (condoms unscrolled on bananas, dimes held between knees), and especially the tedious ceremonial unwrapping and passing around of presents, the tiny onesies, hand-knit blankies, baby-food grinders.

Dutifully, I showed up at the hospitals to meet the new humans. I kissed their hot snuffling faces, gathered them, all bundled in flannel and terry cloth, into my arms; holding them made me deliciously sleepy and relaxed. But it didn't make me want one of my own.

"You should have a baby," a friend reported the day after giving birth, "if only to feel the great tidal wave of love that crashes through you."

I didn't want to feel such love for someone else. I still wanted to be the object of that tidal wave.

I knew better than to voice this, of course. Ashamed of such a selfish, infantile craving, I kept it secret. But I knew that so long as I begrudged a child love and attention, I would never be a good parent, and it was wise not to become one.

Meanwhile, these tiny newcomers changed my friendships. Anything a baby did—chortle, fart, emit a piercing scream—trumped whatever we adults were talking about. Conversations, once our great pleasure, were now sound bites snatched between negotiations over toys and candy. One friend who lived forty miles away had me over for dinner— her husband was out of town, so we'd have a whole night to talk! Before dessert, she went to put her three-year-old to bed. And never came back. I called out to her a few times, at intervals. In all, I sat at the table for more than an hour, politely refraining from the *pot de crème*.

Then I drove the forty miles home.

With second children, friends disappeared fully into family life. They were inducted into new modes of socializing that I did not envy or wish to join: kiddie birthday parties and group camping trips with other young families and the rare fragment of adult conversation. Even as I grieved the damping off of these long-enjoyed friendships, I was never tempted to join the ranks of motherhood.

I had no interest in having a family or being in one.

For as far back as I can remember, I was nonplussed and somewhat horrified by the family I was born into. In fact, my first clearly articulated thought—it came to me when I was probably two and a half or three, standing in the front yard by the myoporum hedge—had to do with my parents: *Who are these people? Why are they acting that way? And how is it that I've come to live among them?*

I didn't know the word *neurotic*, then. But I had the sense, even so young, that my parents overreacted, that they got too worked up over little things, and their responses were often volatile, frantic, and out of all proportion to the issues at hand.

My mother was a diabetic whose pancreas intermittently produced insulin, which made her moods fluctuate wildly. Trained as a concert pianist at the Oberlin Conservatory, she was bored stiff as a stay-at-home mom. She went back to school for her teaching credential when I was six, and went to work when I was seven. She was less bored then, but far from emotionally stable. Anxiety carbonated her blood. Her voice trembled with self-pity, and she often teetered between fury and sobbing; it took nothing—a child's question, a book out of place—to pitch her over into one or the other. She was quick to feel slights. I once dared to ask if we could go into a department store just one time without her asking to see a manager. She nursed grudges—at one point, she didn't talk to my ten-year-old sister for over two weeks.

Our dinner table was her stage; she told long, ongoing sagas that took place in the faculty rooms of schools where she taught; she detailed the rivalries and jealousies of her hapless colleagues, their bad teaching and awful clothes and miserable marriages or love lives. Nobody met her standards. These nightly installments passed for conversation in our home. I often think I became a writer because for the first fifteen years of my life, I never got a word in edgewise.

We daughters were a continuous source of disappointment to her. My sister was overweight. I had wispy, spiderweb hair. Her disapproval hung in our house like a smell. We somehow could never be the well-groomed, seen-and-never-heard girls she'd imagined. Also, we had likes and dislikes, *wills*, and we wanted things: toys and cereals advertised on TV, trendy clothes, permission to go to a friend's house. Our desires, and often our very presence, annoyed and inconvenienced her.

She could not abide (let alone find amusement in) any of our quirks of personality, or preferences, or aversions.

I told her about my terrible cramps when I started menstruating; she wouldn't believe me. *She'd* never had cramps.

My father was distant, uninvolved, mild enough for long stretches, only to explode into violent verbal rages if milk was spilled, or we asked for spending money, or, heaven forbid, he found coins on the floor. We neither knew nor cared about money, he'd yell, and how hard he had to work to support us, and how expensive we were. Periodically, he totted up how much he'd spent on us, and how much we'd cost him in the long run, and announced these hair-raising sums to us as debts we could barely imagine or ever begin to repay.

As elementary school teachers, both my parents were devoted to their work. My mother, especially, took a great interest in her students, at least the best ones. Every fall, before the start of the semester, she would review the cumulative reports of her incoming students, and she would call out the highest IQs in her class. 152! 148! 160! She loved best the challenge of a bright but unresponsive or underperforming student. "I must figure out how to reach Arnold! . . . I haven't reached Arnold yet. . . . I think I finally reached Arnold today!"

My sister and I had decent IQs, too. But my mother never even tried "reaching" us. In fact, neither parent showed any interest in our schoolwork (although a B in any subject would get us grounded).

They took no interest, either, in how we filled the hours after school, beyond discouraging us from making friends with the neighborhood kids, as they were "lower class" and not intelligent enough. I ignored my mother's disapproval and ran with a neighborhood gang whenever I could. Friends became my consolation, my refuge, but I had to meet them on their turf. If they ever came over to my house, they usually declined to come back. My parents' incessant bickering discomfited them, as did my mother's hovering, her abrupt manner and pointed questions ("So tell me, Mary, does your mother allow *you* to keep your room so messy?"). None of my friends could tolerate the tense atmosphere in our house. The chimes of psychic pain.

Home was a place I was always alone.

My sister, who was two years older, retreated into her room early on. There, she practiced the violin, studied, and ate compulsively in secret. (Discovering the balm of food at age six, she has said, was a great moment in her life.)

Alone, I read. I took apart toys and my lamp, my miniature sewing machine, then my mother's Singer, and reassembled them. One evening, I took a project outside to the end of our driveway to work under the streetlight. I was eight, I think, and with some odd scraps of Naugahyde, cardboard, a stapler, and scissors, I endeavored to make shoes. A neighbor, out for a walk after work, stood and observed me for a long time as I measured and cut. I remember this vividly because it was the most prolonged and focused adult attention I'd ever experienced.

My sister would later dub our parents' strategy "strict neglect."

They did not know how to play with us, or be close, or converse amicably, without criticism. But they did want us well educated, and they exposed us to a wide range of experience. We had music lessons, swimming lessons; my sister learned to ride. There was never any question but that the two of us would go to college. We also did many things "as a family": on weekends, we went to museums, concerts, good movies and plays; we camped and took summerlong driving trips (to Alaska, to Guatemala, all across Canada). Eventually, my father built a cabin in the Sierras for weekend use. From the outside, our family looked adventurous, fun loving. Were we more convivial, happier, in those tents, cars, campers, and cabin? Rarely. In close quarters, our mother and her moods still dominated, and we girls withdrew, each into her own solitude.

My parents blithely acknowledged the discrepancy between how they dealt with their students and how they dealt with us. Countless times one or the other declared, "Parents are amateurs, but *teachers* are professionals."

Indeed, it was deep in the intimate, hidden recesses of family that their volatility and emotional immaturity raged unchecked.

Many times, my mother declared that if my father ever so much as laid a finger on her, she'd leave him on the spot. However, both parents slapped and spanked with abandon—flat-handed wallops to the face that juttered my teeth; they used rulers and hairbrushes and flyswatters, badminton racquets, whatever was in reach. Someone gave my sister and me an Eskimo yo-yo and I refused to thank her; I knew I'd feel its broad flat smack soon enough. (I did.) Through high school, I could tell by the way my mother entered the house when she came home from work—the swing of the door, the drop of her handbag, the tenor of her sighs—how ill-tempered she was, and therefore, the likelihood of my being struck in the next few minutes. She would come to my room and accuse me of something—not hanging up my clothes or forgetting to put down the lid of the laundry hamper. I would deny it or try to explain; that would be "talking back" and would earn a slap or worse.

My parents' theory of corporal punishment distinguished between hitting and beating. They were very open about, even proud of, their method. Lower-class people beat and left marks. Middle-class people hit hard enough to sting and humiliate, and "to bring on a catharsis," as my father liked to say, but not so hard that they bruised. Lingering redness didn't count. I occasionally had a dappling of black-and-blue marks on my upper arms where my mother's fingers dug in, but these didn't count either.

Now, many people come from homes where the physical abuse far exceeded the slaps and spanks and arm grabbing at my house, yet they still want kids and set out to correct the mistakes their parents made, and even consciously address the intergenerational patterns of violence. I have friends from families long ridden with addiction, abuse, and poverty who have become loving, responsible, sober parents and made safe, calm homes for their children.

So why did neither my sister nor I ever want to "do it right" and live in a family of our own making? My sister knew all along that she never wanted children—although she's a violin teacher who works with and delights in children daily. I never took such a defiant or conclusive stance. Day to day, the desire for children never quite formed and surfaced, and certainly never to the degree where I eyed the town drunk or the box boy.

What kept the desire from even taking shape?

A friend who grew up with an alcoholic father said that despite her father's disease and the toll it took on the family, children were wanted and cherished in their home. This friend has two beloved children, now adults.

My mother clearly had wanted children; as a somewhat brittle diabetic, she had them even knowing that pregnancy and birth could endanger her life. But at a certain point— once we acquired wills—she had no idea what to do with us. I must have heard her say a hundred times, whenever she saw or held a baby, "Don't you wish you could just pickle them at this stage?"

I was ten when my sister and I went into her room to see her stretched out on the bed, refusing the sugared orange juice my father urged her to drink. She was "low": a sudden, unpredictable infusion of insulin had sent her blood sugar plummeting. "Who are these goddamn children?" she cried to my father, slurring her words as if drunk. "Make them go away. I don't want any children. Get rid of them."

I heard this not with surprise or even deep pain, but with a sense of relief. Finally. Finally, what I'd long suspected had been spoken. She had thought she wanted kids, but once she had them, she really didn't. We failed to bring her happiness.

It seemed certain that children wouldn't bring me happiness either.

My experience of living in my family had deeply instilled a sense that behind the closed doors of a family's home, all respect disappeared; disapproval, anger, and other emotions ran unchecked, and a domestic form of war prevailed, with war's oscillations between overt violence and tense calm.

Even as I learned that not all families were like this, I didn't trust myself not to re-create what I had known.

I believe it was no coincidence that I waited to marry until it was biologically impossible for me to have a family.

I left to go away to college a month after I turned sixteen, and I never lived at home again. I decided I wanted to be a writer, and that became my focus and passion, although it would be years before I settled down into regular work habits. My college career was spotty; restless and discontented, I attended three different schools. But my focus on writing was constant; I went to graduate school for an MFA, and spent the rest of my twenties trying to write publishable prose.

In my thirties I began to scrape together a living writing freelance articles while struggling to write my first novel. Again and again, I fell hard for remote, often unavailable men and tried, unsuccessfully, to make them love me. Love was my grand distraction. My drinking slowly slid into excess, until, at thirty-four, I had a moment of clarity: I realized that I could improve neither my writing nor myself if I was getting drunk every night.

That year I went into therapy, got sober, and landed steady work, which together set me firmly on the long, twisting ascent to my present contentment. En route, I abandoned my efforts to make the disinterested love me, and I learned to recognize and appreciate the genuinely interested. I published countless articles for magazines and newspapers and, finally, in my early forties, the first of several novels. Writing absorbed me. I felt lucky to have such a passion. If a certain restlessness or emptiness assailed me in all those years of dwindling fertility, I never perceived it as a biological imperative to reproduce, but as part of the ups and downs of a creative life.

Several times, I voiced concern over my childlessness to several writer friends of mine, women who had kids. "Don't do it!" they chorused. "Write unimpeded!" I didn't "take" their advice so much as I used it to justify my ongoing childless state.

I always assumed that someday, at some vague, distant point, I'd become a fit and willing parent. With years of therapy, I did outgrow my resentment toward and impatience with kids, and I got a handle on that driving need for parental attention and love; I accepted, with some sorrow, that it was too late to get that particular package—your chance for it comes only once in life. I understood more about my parents, too, about diabetes and mood swings, and about how my father grew up in a home where bruising beatings and potentially mortal combat took place.

I became more able and even somewhat willing to be a parent, but by the time that happened, and by the time I met a man who might be a wonderful father, we were too old and, as he likes to say, too set in our ways. And just because I was a little more willing and a lot more able to be a parent didn't mean I was itching to become one. Or could. Indeed, two months before our wedding—I was fifty-two—I stopped menstruating and developed hot flashes: a new version of the blushing bride.

I would say that originally, I was childless due to damage. But ultimately, I did come to the place of choosing. After all, my husband and I could have adopted or possibly undergone one of those newfangled fertility procedures. But there were many other considerations, then. Did we want to be seventy when our child graduated from high school? And that's assuming we got right on it—did we want to spend the first months of marriage meeting with adoption lawyers? If we waited five years, did we want to be seventy-five on graduation day?

I have no regrets. I have been grateful for the freedom not to have children—it is a relatively new freedom, unknown to most women throughout history. At times, I feel like a pioneer, a woman who has had access to countless new opportunities, including the chance to craft a life best suited to her own skills and temperament. Here, I stand in contrast to my mother, who took up marriage and family by default, because the job for which she'd actually been trained, concert pianist, did not exist for women.

It's not as if I consciously chose a career over having children, or that my career particularly benefitted from my childlessness. The time I didn't spend on raising kids, I squandered on love affairs and staring out windows; it took me many years after grad school to establish discipline in my work. But I did get to build a life around writing, and it became a very good life, one in which I was able to work through my lonely, difficult, contradictory childhood without unconsciously inflicting all that residual pain on innocents.

While writing this essay, I discussed it with the old friend who warned me about wrecking my karma when I was pregnant so long ago—she and I have known each other now for forty-seven years. She'd forgotten her warning, because this time, talking about how poor we all were and how lost I was back then, she exclaimed, "Thank God you didn't have that baby!"

What maternal stirrings I've had, I feel, have been satisfactorily redirected. Some of those snuffling, hot babies I kissed in their first swaddlings are now adult friends. I have friends who are in grammar school, and my favorite movie date for the past six or seven years is presently a junior in high school. I also teach creative writing to undergraduates, and work closely with several younger women writers.

The fortune-teller I saw at twenty-five proved correct in all her predictions. I was poor for decades, finally getting comfortable in my fifties. In my twenties and early thirties, I grappled with alcoholism—a serious but not necessarily fatal disease; I have been sober now for twenty-six years. And I know, too, on which side the fortune-teller's cosmic source fell in the debate over when life begins. The one child sent to me by fate, I chose not to have.

I can live with that.

SAVE YOURSELF

by

Danielle Henderson

MY GRANDMA USED to walk us to school. She'd show up at our apartment on her way to work, when the light was just peeking over the edge of the windowsill in the bedroom I shared with my brother. I imagine she and my mother passed each other like ghosts, my grandma pumping her small, thick legs up the stairs as my mother glided down, on her way to the first shift in the tiny building where she would solder small silver wires to large green plates all day. My grandmother gently shook my brother and me awake and guided us by the shoulders into the kitchen, where we would stand in front of the already warm oven and get dressed. "Gas is cheaper than electricity," she said, Depression-era thinking still lingering in 1984.

School was only a couple of streets away, but no one let

their kids walk alone after the movie about Adam Walsh's kidnapping and murder had aired on TV the year before. My brother usually peeled off and ran ahead to join his class, but I always stayed by my grandma's side, kicking through the dry red leaves on the ground.

"I'm never going to college, and I'm never having babies," I said to her one day.

When she tells this story now she laughs the same way she did then, the sound deep and sudden like the blast of a baritone horn. I heard that laugh just above my head as I kept walking, leaves sticking to the Velcro-fastened Punky Brewster sneakers firmly attached to my seven-year-old feet. "Oh yeah? What makes you say that?" she chuckled, humoring me.

"College is like jail, and babies are gross," I said, resolute.

"Well, you don't know what you're going to do in life yet, Dani. You'll probably change your mind."

"No," I said, "I won't."

I did go to college, and then graduate school, but thirty years have passed since that conversation, and in that time I've never wanted to have children. I harbor no deep biological urge, no longing, no worry over who will visit me or wipe my ass when I'm elderly. If the biological clock were an actual organ, mine would be as useless as an appendix. Since I've always known I didn't want children, I never agonized over whether or not to have them as though it were a major life decision. Children were just never going to fit into my life.

Strangers ask me all the time about my reasons for not having children, mostly when they see that I love kids. I always engage children on their level, and I like to give them chances to show off by asking about their favorite books or letting them tell me incredibly long-winded stories full of "ums" or "and thens." I use my considerable height to my advantage and constantly hike the kids in my life up on my shoulders and ask them to steer the ship by telling me where to walk or run. I like to be the first person to teach them fart jokes, and I always indulge every knock-knock joke, even that endless one about the orange. There's a near-universal assumption that women who don't want to have children fundamentally dislike children, but that's often not the case. I think kids are great; they're curious about the world in a way that reminds me to be interested and open. I had a lucrative babysitting career when I was a teenager; I love running around with my nieces and nephews in the summer when I'm trying to teach them how to skateboard, or they're trying to teach me how to work the controls on their new robotic toys.

I recognize the work and sacrifice that goes into being a good parent and I think I'd be well suited to the task; though the idea of pushing a baby out of my body has always seemed painful and ruinous to me, I'm not afraid of babies. I'm not afraid of all the things you have to do to keep them alive, and I think I'd be able to do it all without worrying about them constantly. I don't think babies need thousands of dollars' worth of toys or equipment to be happy and well-adjusted, and I already stay awake until three A.M. most nights, bleary-eyed but focused as I work on projects or finish writing essays like these. Parenting doesn't freak me out. But I spent the majority of my formative years healing from what felt to me like bad parenting, which made me realize that sometimes your willingness to be a parent isn't enough. Sometimes love runs out. It took me a long time to figure out how to fill my life with the love my parents didn't seem able to give me. I decided to take the love I'd have for a child and give it to myself instead.

My mother left us at my grandparents' house during the winter school break when I was ten years old. It didn't sink in right away that she wasn't coming back. My brother and I didn't even have most of our stuff; all I'd brought were my books for school, a week's worth of clothes, and the relief of knowing that I wouldn't have to be near my stepfather for the next seven days. I barely gave my mom a hug and kiss before I wiggled away and ran up the steps to the front door of my grandparents' duplex. From the couch in the living room, I watched her car turn the corner and disappear out of sight, my stepfather hunched behind the wheel. It scared me to think so at the time, but I was glad to see them go.

The abuse didn't start right away, but my stepfather's presence was disruptive from the moment he moved in. He came home at all hours of the night, and we often woke up to him in the living room watching TV or making breakfast in the kitchen. He didn't care about the rules of the house—he was loud when we were forbidden to be, and he always slammed the door, even when he supposedly wasn't mad. He made me feel lonely, dominating my mother's time and constantly telling me to go somewhere else to play when all I wanted to do was be around my mom. Before that, for as long as I could remember, it had always been only the three of us—my mom, my brother, and me. I didn't like waking up to this stranger in our home every day. My mom didn't date much and my world was small—outside of our apartment, I went to school; to Hanley's five-and-dime on the corner to get candy on Fridays; to the Grand Union grocery store; to the Four Seasons diner, where we would sometimes go for breakfast to sit at the counter and spin on the vinyl stools; and to my grandparents' house. I saw the same people everywhere, and I was rarely in the presence of people I didn't know.

My mother was a great mom in the beginning, even though we didn't have much. My parents split up a couple of months before I was born. This was easy for them; they weren't married, and my great-grandmother paid for my pregnant mom and one-year-old brother, Cory, to take the bus home to Greenwood Lake, New York, after my mom ran away to North Carolina with my dad, her high school sweetheart. My brother and I lived with our grandparents for a year while my mom got back on her feet, then moved into a small two-bedroom apartment over a deli in the middle of our very small town. I didn't know what the word *welfare* meant, but I did notice that the money my mom used to pay for groceries looked like the money in our Monopoly game, and our milk came in a powder-filled box instead of a carton of liquid like it did at my friend Erin's house. It was 1984, and the first rumblings of the personal computer era could be heard all around us; my mom worked the early shift at a small electronics company. She wanted to be home with us after school, but sometimes she also worked a job at night cleaning offices while the next-door neighbor made sure my brother and I got to bed on time. Though we were on public assistance, my mom saw welfare as a stopover on the way to the rest of our lives and was very careful about saving where possible. No amount of crying or complaining on my part ever resulted in my getting a Barbie doll for my birthday, but we had enough to eat most of the time and never had to worry about where we would sleep at night.

Everything changed when she met my stepfather. It was the summer I turned seven, and Cory and I spent it in California with my aunt in order to give my mom a break and a chance to work more overtime. My aunt flew back with us in August, and when we got home, our apartment looked amazing. My mom had somehow made enough money to buy a new couch and end tables, and brand-new furniture for our bedrooms. Instead of the black metal bed frame that had been passed down through three generations, I had a white wooden frame with a small headboard, a tiny group of colorful flowers painted right in the middle. My dresser matched the bed frame and had brassy pulls that made a tinkling sound whenever I opened or closed the drawers. Our new couch was a pastel-striped affair with three overstuffed cushions pushing out from the back, one space for each of us. My mother was so proud she couldn't stop smiling, couldn't wait to show us everything.

"Tomorrow we'll all go to the city and buy some new school clothes," she said.

We lived an hour outside of Manhattan, where my mom had grown up in Harlem, and it was a treat every time we got to go there. Even now, the hair on my arms stands at attention when I round the corner for the Lincoln Tunnel and the entire skyline opens up. Inside the tunnel, I relish those quiet moments underwater before spilling out into midtown, a party already in full swing. When we got to Macy's that day, a man shopping in the shoe department started talking to my aunt right away. When he asked for her phone number, she sucked her teeth, rolled her eyes, and walked away to look at a different pair of shoes.

Then he turned to my mother. He was the tallest man I'd ever seen, even with his slight hunch, and had short-cropped hair that was slightly receding in the front. He wore jeans and a light colored T-shirt, and his eyes darted around like he was waiting for someone to sneak attack him in a never-ending game of tag. I was too far away to hear what he said to my mom, but she opened up like a flower when he approached her, and a week later he was sleeping on our new couch and using our new plates.

I'm not sure when my mom realized how much trouble he was, or why, once she found out, she didn't throw him out and change the locks on the door. I don't understand why she didn't protect us. Later, Cory and I would realize that he used drugs, but at the time all we knew was that we had to be very quiet when we came home from school because he was always sleeping and would hit us if we woke him up. We knew that our furniture was starting to disappear, and my mom was always yelling at him about money. We knew that my mom switched to the night shift at the electronics company so she could earn a little extra doing another job during the day. After I went to bed, this man who'd never left our house after that weekend at Macy's would hover in my door in the darkness.

The Macy's man lived with us for three years. Then came the winter break when my mother married him. She dropped my brother and me off at my grandparents' house and moved with her new husband to his mother's apartment in the Bronx. We didn't see my mom for two years after we watched her drive away. She called sometimes, but what could I possibly say to her on the phone to make her come back? My grandparents had retired by then and moved into a two-bedroom duplex, and our arrival split the house awkwardly. I shared a room with my grandmother, and my brother shared a room with my grandfather. They traded in their queen-size bed for two twin beds. Life at my grandparents' house was easier; both of them went back to work to support us and we always had food in the house. During the week, after we finished our homework, we were allowed to play with the new Nintendo they got us, and on the weekends my grandmother would play Monopoly and Parcheesi with us. It was better than living with the Macy's man, but I still missed my mom and our life before him.

I'd never wanted to have children. Even before my stepfather unleashed so much chaos into our lives, parenting had always struck me as an extreme pain in the ass, a total time suck. But watching my mother fail so completely at protecting us didn't make motherhood look like a job worth having even for those who said they wanted it. Motherhood was always difficult for her and her struggle was always right there on the surface. Through her I learned that motherhood has no guarantees—you didn't have to love your kids, and you didn't even have to stay with them and finish the job. My mom worked more than anyone I knew and was often testy and short-tempered with us. I got the feeling that we were a complete drag—she worked so hard to take care of us, and then she barely wanted to be around us. We got to play and explore, but she never had time to herself. My grandparents had been fantastic when we were not living with them, but when we moved in and shook up their lives, they started to take on that tiredness I'd seen in my mom, too. Through my mom's parenting I learned that there was more pain and hurt than there was joy and happiness in the world, and it scared me to death to think of bringing a brand-new person into that heady mix. How could I ever be sure that I would do a better job? What if her failure was genetic, and I was worse?

Recovering from my childhood required a lot of emotional heavy lifting. During the three-year stretch when I lived with my stepfather, my grandparents had been kept at arm's length. They didn't know the extent of the abuse I'd suffered, and when Cory and I moved in and they became our guardians, I couldn't find a way to tell them. I wouldn't see my first therapist until I was almost twenty years old. I spent most of my teen years feeling suicidal and disconnected from the world. I had friends, but the shame of what had happened to me made me feel isolated. I did some after-school things like drum corps and softball, but I mostly stayed in my room and read or watched TV while I was sewing, a favorite hobby. My mom went on to have three more kids with my stepfather, a new family, and she eventually came back to see us when I was thirteen years old, but it was only a visit and she had no plans to take us back. I had already decided I wanted nothing to do with her; I just wanted to get out of my small town and get to a place so far away I never had to see my mother again.

It's not fair to say that my mother is the sole reason I don't want to have children. Like I said, I've never had those biological pangs. I could have had the best mother in the world and still relegated childbearing and raising to the list of things I'll never do. But she added a layer of uncertainty to the whole endeavor, which makes me wonder if the nature-versus-nurture debate is as black-and white as it seems. A lot of people who had terrible childhoods have kids to prove that they can do a better job, or to fix some cosmic rift by being the parents they needed to their own children. I sometimes wonder why I fall into the category of people who respond to their own crappy childhoods by never wanting to have kids. It's possible that I'm not very brave; you have to have a lot of hope and faith that you've somehow learned everything your family was supposed to teach you but didn't. You have to tell yourself you'll be able to avoid the pitfalls you grew up with. But, even then, you create new pitfalls. I negotiate the terms of my life every day and work hard to maintain an emotional status quo that I had to create from scratch. That's hard to do with a child in tow.

"But you're so good with kids," my friends say. "You know you'd be a good mom just because you'll never make the same mistakes *your* mom did. Children have a way of healing you."

That sounds like a spectacularly shitty premise to me, and way too much pressure to put on a child. In an attempt to piece myself back together, I was in therapy for most of my twenties. I would later go to graduate school for English literature and gender studies, but in between I moved around the country a lot, including to Alaska, and tried my hand at several different careers—barista, bookstore employee, bartender. Finally, I figured out that I didn't need to have my mother in my life to feel deeply loved, and that I could choose what kind of relationship I wanted to cultivate with her (which, as it turns out, is no relationship at all).

As a woman who chooses to be childless, I generally have just one problem: other adults. Living in a culture where women are assumed to prioritize motherhood above all else and where a woman's personal choices are often considered matters of public discussion means everyone thinks they have the right to discuss my body and my choices, so anyone who is curious about my lack of spawn feels the right to march right on over and ask me about it. If I'm feeling generous, I laugh off their questions by putting the onus on myself and my perceived lack of certain capabilities. "Oh, my mom was really terrible at being a mom and it seems like a hard job," I'll say. When I'm feeling less than generous, I ask, "Why do you want to know?" or tell them that not every woman wants to have kids. Sometimes a discussion will stem from there, but most of the time I just want people to realize that they're not only breaching my privacy but also putting their flawed assumptions directly in my lap.

As bothered as I am by having to defend my decision, I'm more incensed that people think they have the right to ask. That's because to ask me why I don't have children is really to ask me to unpack my complicated history with parenting, or to try to explain something I've felt since I found out where babies come from. Since people often ask this question as casually as they ask, "What brought you to Seattle?" I'm expected to answer it in an equally casual manner, which I am unable and unwilling to do.

I admire women who look at the rigors of parenting and decide they're just not cut out for it, or just don't want to try, and I wish that we had more conversations about childlessness that didn't force us to approach them from such a defensive place. I'm also sensitive to the fact that there are plenty of women in the world who want children and are unable to have them naturally, or women who have miscarried, often more than once, on their journey to parenthood. It seems hostile and uncaring to have a conversation about motherhood that is rooted in selfishness when so many women are unable to walk down that road.

When I started dating in my early twenties, I let my partners know right away that I did not want children. I was always quick to broach that subject with anyone I dated seriously, not wanting to go further if we weren't on the same page. For the most part they didn't care—men in their twenties tend not to be too focused on when or whether they want to become fathers. In fact, I never felt like it was something I had to explain until I met my husband. He was an easygoing artist from Rhode Island who spent most of his time reading and talking about comic books on the Internet, and we were friends for several years before we started dating. He has always known that I didn't want to have children, but now that so much time had gone by and we were facing the world together as partners as well as friends, I was worried that we would disagree on this fundamental topic. What if he had changed his mind? We had a short engagement; there were only five weeks between the day we decided to get married and our Halloween Day wedding. During that time, in the midst of my grad school teaching schedule and generally hectic life, it occurred to me that I should check in with him again about the kid thing.

My timing tends to be rotten; when I have something on my mind I just blurt it out, so one night while we were having dinner on the couch I said, "So I still don't want to have kids." He looked at me and smiled, and in his incredibly chill way told me it was fine. He said that he'd never made plans to have kids. Then he joked that he might have kids he never even knew about and that they could show up at our door any minute. I told him I was worried that he might change his mind in the future and be saddled with me, but he laughed and said we could just get divorced if he ever changed his mind. Some might see that as harsh, but I saw it as honest—and not all that likely to come to fruition. In the end, he doesn't think he wants children, but he does know he wants to be with me, so we're hanging our hopes on that hook.

As with overcoming my childhood abuse, choosing not to become a parent means that I've had to redefine my concept of family. I consider my family to be a cobbled-together group of friends and people I'm related to, all defined by the fact that I can count on them. My grandmother is my family and so is my older brother; my husband is my family for sure, and through him I've been able to count his mother, father, and brother among my family. My best friends are my family— Alexis, whom I've known since sixth-grade science with Mr. Waleski; Sarah, whom I met through blogging when we were aimless twentysomethings; and Sandra, whom I met at a concert in New York City when I was twenty-two and who immediately felt like a missing link to happiness.

I am the person responsible for my grandmother's well-being; I manage her medical bills, arrange all her monthly payments, call to check in with her doctor about his plan for her to manage her diabetes, and fix her iPad when she wants to upgrade her games. She lives across the country in New York and I am in Seattle, but I'm the one caring for her—not my mother. As I watch her age, I want to shield her against anything that makes her feel scared or unmoored, and I can't help but wonder who will do the same for me. Though I've often said I'm not afraid to get old without the built-in support system most people find in their children because I've created my own *chosen* support system, the truth is that I won't know for sure until I get there. What I do know is that I have nieces and nephews whom I'm proud to see growing into interesting, thoughtful people. I have friends whose children I adore—even children I haven't met yet. As I write this essay, three of my closest friends are pregnant after years of uncertainty as to whether they even wanted to have kids. I call all these buns-in-ovens "Porkchop," and I look forward to passing along my own wisdom and being part of their lives.

Those who hear my story might be tempted to assume that my desire to be childless is rooted in loss—the loss of my mother's protection and loyalty, the loss of faith in family, the loss of childhood itself. But to me, the lack of desire to have a child is innate. It exists outside of my control. It is simply who I am and I can take neither credit nor blame for all that it may or may not signify. But the decision to honor that desire, to find a way to be whole on my own terms even if it means facing the judgment, scorn, and even pity of mainstream society, is a victory. It's a victory I celebrate every day.

Every day, I try to be my own parent—the parent I never had. Every day, I learn new ways to treat myself with compassion and patience. I've made a life that centers around writing and that gives me freedom to travel and to construct my day around my moods and thoughts. Yoga helps me alleviate stress and get out of my head a bit. A couple times a week, I like to sit and have coffee with my neighbors on the back porch. We catch up on each other's lives and talk about the world, or our place in this city we love so much. My husband and I spend a lot of time together, reading or going out to eat or just talking about the dreams and goals we have for the future, like buying and renovating a house, adopting a dog, or retiring in Paris. My childhood was so inconsistent that I never expected normalcy, and it's enough for me to be able to have time and space to be good to myself and the people around me. Children are nice, but I decided to save myself instead.

THE TROUBLE WITH HAVING IT ALL

by

Pam Houston

TWO HOURS AFTER President Barack Obama was reelected, I sat on the top floor of the SFO parking lot in the pouring rain listening to his acceptance speech and bawling my eyes out. I had a ticket on the red-eye to Houston, connecting to Indianapolis, where I had a three-day engagement, reading to, teaching, and getting to know the creative writing students at Butler University. It was just under an hour till flight time, but I was going to sit in that car until the president finished speaking even if it meant I missed my plane. He finished, and I made a run for the terminal, still crying. It was all I could do not to hug the six other people in the security line, as well as all the TSA employees.

What I felt most strongly that night was relief. Relief that the attempts to keep African Americans away from the polls had ultimately not been successful. Relief that people weren't, in the end, quite as stupid as Karl Rove gave them credit for. Relief that in 2012 in the United States of America it was still true that no amount of money could buy an election. Relief, above all, that the people who spent the 2012 presidential campaign waging a war on women and their various freedoms had—at least in this round—lost again.

At Butler University the students were smart, engaged, and engaging. At dinner, the young women did all the talking, mapping out their lives and expressing their hearts' desires, while the young men sat quietly, some combination of shy and polite, paying close attention to the women as if they might have something to learn. In honor of the election results, one young woman—the liveliest at the table, and the funniest—was wearing all red, white, and blue, and by that I mean that nearly every piece of clothing and jewelry she had on was *all three* colors. She even had all three colors of fingernail polish on every fingernail, and each nail was appliquéd with a tiny American flag.

Every woman at the table had big dreams about her career; most also intended to have children, but not for a while, not until they had written novels and won Pulitzer Prizes and visited fifty or sixty countries and learned how to surf. "I want to have it all" was an expression that flew around the table, and it was clear that these women had every intention of doing so.

One of the quieter women spoke with admiration about her sister who lived in New York, making a quarter of a million dollars a year at Lehman Brothers while raising two children under five. The sister managed, even with her sixty-hour workweek, to post to her home blog every night about the cookies she had found the time to bake for the kids or the handmade yak-wool couch covers she had ordered from a Kiva start-up in Tibet.

"My fiancé wants to start trying for kids right after graduation," said another woman, glancing down at the chip of diamond on her left hand.

Two kids was the agreed-upon hoped-for number around the table, except for one woman who wanted "at least three," and another who was an only child and enjoyed the special treatment that had afforded her.

I noticed Ms. Red White and Blue had fallen a little silent when the talk turned to children. "And you?" I said, to re-engage her, missing the way her big laugh had become the timpani completing the symphony of female voices at the table. "Where do you stand on children?"

She raised one eyebrow a full inch above the level of the other and said, "Not if hell froze over and hair grew out of the palm of my hand."

Our eyes locked for a minute and I felt the corners of my mouth rise involuntarily.

"I used to feel that way," said the soft-spoken woman, "but

my sister says having a baby is the only way a woman will ever stop being all about herself."

"The worst thing of all," said the only child, "would be not to do it, and then realize you had totally missed out."

"I don't know," said Ms. Red White and Blue, not aggressively. "I'm pretty sure that having it *all* might *not* be. I think maybe having it all is chopping yourself into too many little pieces, taking care of everybody's needs except your own."

The other girls leapt to reassure her, "Oh, you'll feel differently when you get older. Sometime around thirty your hormones will kick in." They said this with great authority, as if they weren't all nineteen themselves.

"They won't," she said, without a hint of rancor, and I believed her, because take away thirty years and the American flag nail appliqués and Ms. Red White and Blue was me.

I am fifty-two years old, a writer, a teacher, and a traveler in the old-fashioned sense of the word, meaning I have been to seventy countries and I don't really feel I can claim a destination until I've gotten lost, gotten arrested, or thrown up. I got my first period the same month the Supreme Court ratified *Roe v. Wade*, and perhaps it was therefore my destiny not to have children.

I never wanted a child—that much was clear—and yet I had lots of friends who said they didn't want them but then all of a sudden had them, which here in the first world, post *Roe v. Wade*, must mean that I didn't want them even more than my friends didn't.

The closest I ever came to wanting a child was while writing an article more than a decade ago questioning my own adamancy on the subject in response to all the people—many but not all of them strangers—who told me, uninvited, that I was in some kind of denial. But by the time I finished the article, I was pretty sure I wasn't. Ten years later I'm even more sure. Or at least confident that if I am in denial, I am never going to know. These same people always told me that I would make a great mother, even if they had only known me for five minutes. For all they knew (as we like to say around my house in response to uninformed assumptions), I could have been fucking the dog.

It wasn't all that long ago that we thought Mitt Romney had a decent chance of being elected president, and it seemed clear that at least one of his missions in that role would be to overturn *Roe v. Wade*. A lot of crazy things were said during that election year, but perhaps none of them crazier than when Representative Todd Akin said that if a woman experienced a "legitimate" rape, she wouldn't get pregnant because the female body has ways of "shutting that whole thing down." It is hard to enumerate all the ways Akin's suggestion is insidious, but let's try. First, his comment blows right past the usual accusation that women "ask" to be raped by their provocative clothing and behavior and moves on to suggest that any rape victim who didn't take nefarious pleasure in the actual procedure could avoid abortion altogether by employing her witchy womanly ways to terminate the resulting pregnancy. Abortion would become unnecessary, except perhaps in the case of a very weak woman whose secret powers were not cutting the mustard, inversely proving, in Todd Akin logic, that she had not been "legitimately" raped. And what, one shudders to ask, does that mean, precisely? Is it "illegitimate" rape if you wore fishnet stockings to the bar? Is it illegitimate rape if your car broke down in a shitty part of town? How about if it's all in the family? Does Uncle Charlie get one free go at the twins at the New Year's Eve party? Is it illegitimate rape if the rapist is your dad?

In the 1970s and '80s it had not yet become critically unfashionable for writers to be concerned about the environment. We didn't even know about global warming, and yet the average citizen—at least in the circles I ran in—felt considerably more pressure to reduce the impact she was making on the planet's ecology than she seems to feel today. A woman could say she didn't want to have children because she didn't want to contribute to the overpopulation of the earth— that already teeming planet—and while some people may not have believed her, it was an acceptable, even admirable, way for her to take a pass. My friend the writer Terry Tempest Williams made such a claim at the time, which caused a stir, for obvious reasons, in the Mormon community from which she originates. I looked up to Terry—I still do—and loved the natural world with a similar passion. I wanted nothing to do with diapers made out of petroleum products, wanted to take no responsibility for one more dream home being built on wild land.

I have a photo of Terry and me at the Salt Lake City Book Festival in 1992 where, between us, we don't look drinking age. We are sitting at a table behind stacks of the newly released *Cowboys Are My Weakness* and *Coyote's Canyon*, and behind our eyes I see nothing but excitement and wildness and delight. We are living the lives our mothers' generation couldn't even imagine, and we know it. We are architects of our own destiny. We are free.

The feminism of a few decades ago was far less full of booby traps for the woman who wanted to claim it as a stance than it is in today's superspecialized jargon-laden academicized version. It was far less likely to strike itself to death over semantics like an overagitated snake. Nineteen seventies feminism declared its ideals in simple sentences one could either agree with or not: A woman had the right to be an artist. A woman had the right to run for office. A woman had the right to attend—for instance—Dartmouth College. A woman had the right not to make babies. A woman had the right not to be a wife.

My women's studies teacher at Denison University in 1980 wore IUDs as earrings. I had such a giant crush on her it can still make me blush. Nan Nowik was tall and elegant and upright in her feminism. In her class we read "The Yellow Wallpaper," *Sula, Love Medicine, The Bluest Eye*. She accused us daily—no doubt justifiably—of being slaves to the dominant paradigm, by which she meant, of course, the Patriarchy. She was strange, and she wanted to know in what ways we were strange, and in the super-prepped-out frat-party world of Denison in those days, she was a lifeline. Nan Nowik didn't once tell us that having it all meant we would win the National Book Award and then give birth to 2.3 babies. Nan Nowik would have found the idea of a blog about baking cookies absurd.

These days it is widely assumed that a woman who doesn't want to have children is reacting—perhaps overreacting—to damage that was done to her in her childhood. I can't refute this claim with any certainty, because the usual trifecta of abuse (alcohol, sexual, physical) did indeed define my own. And yet I become, as I age, less and less convinced that is the whole story. In the first place, thirty years of teaching creative writing has proven to me that my childhood story is as common as a two-car garage. In the second place, I've been working my whole life to heal those old wounds and, frankly, I don't feel that damaged anymore.

Try this on. What if I didn't want to have babies because I loved my job too much to compromise it, or because serious travel makes me feel *in relation* to the world in an utterly essential way? What if I've always liked the looks of my own life much better than those of the ones I saw around me? What if, given the option, I would prefer to accept an assignment to go trekking for a month in the kingdom of Bhutan than spend that same month folding onesies? What if I simply like dogs a whole lot better than babies? What if I have become sure that personal freedom is the thing I hold most dear?

Some of my closest friends love being mothers, live, to a certain extent, to be mothers. It has been the single most challenging and rewarding endeavor of their lives. Others of my friends don't like it that much, thought they would like it better than they do, are counting the days till the last kid goes off to college so they can turn their attention to their own dreams. A few friends pretend to love it, but everyone within twelve square miles can hear them grinding their teeth. Still others pretend motherhood is the world's biggest hassle and yet you can tell they love it deep down. And then there are my childless friends, who fit right into corresponding categories: the ones who love childlessness, the ones who regret it, and the ones who pretend to be in the opposite camp from the one they're in. A childless friend recently said to me, "I will never regret not having children. What I regret is that I live in a world where in spite of everything, that decision is still not quite okay."

It seems unreasonable, not to mention sexist, to suggest that because all women have the biological capacity to have children, they all should; and that those who don't are either in denial or psychologically damaged. My score on the LSAT indicates that I have the mental capacity to be a lawyer, but I have not gotten one single letter from a stranger or anyone else telling me that I would make a really great lawyer, that the fact that I am not a lawyer must be related to some deep-seated childhood trauma, that if I would only straighten up and become a lawyer, I could pay off some unspecified debt to the world.

There are quite a few actualities of contemporary American life that despite all the time I've had to get used to them still stagger my imagination. It staggers my imagination that so many people who are struggling physically and financially are so resistant to the policies that would provide them with affordable health care. It staggers my imagination that an angry teenager can walk into a store and buy a weapon that will fire a hundred rounds of ammunition without reloading, but I can't take my 3.2-ounce bottle of Aveda shampoo on board an airplane embarking on a forty-minute commuter flight. And it staggers my imagination that any woman will vote for a politician who has been up front about wanting to control what does and doesn't happen inside her womb.

In the years since the *Roe v. Wade* ruling, conservative lawmakers in many states have whittled away at it, adding laws about waiting periods, mandatory counseling, parental consent, and, bizarrely, in Indiana, the size of the hall and the doorway through which morning-after pills are distributed. At the time of this writing, six states—Utah, Virginia, Ohio, Louisiana, Missouri, and my state, Colorado—have "trigger" laws on the subject of abortion, meaning that if *Roe v. Wade* were overturned, abortion would become illegal in that state effective immediately. Twenty-three additional states have trigger laws on late-term abortion. Pro-choice activists believe it is only a matter of time before a state writes a bill that effectively dodges the language of *Roe v. Wade*. In 2012, NARAL estimated that if Mitt Romney were elected president, seventeen states would ban abortion within the year.

There are many controversial issues in contemporary American politics where, in spite of my strong feelings, I have the ability to understand and respect the other side. But the notion that we could ever pretend women have real equality in this country when a man as uninformed about basic reproductive gynecology as Mr. Todd Akin could take away my right to decide whether I want to spend a minimum of eighteen years and an average of $235,000 raising a child—not to mention the significant cost to my own dreams and goals or the myriad ways my child might ultimately suffer for my having been denied the ability to make that choice, the ways so many children suffer every day at the hands of their frustrated, stultified mothers—is an absurdity.

Against abortion? the bumper sticker says. *Then don't have one!* And in 2015, that should be the end of that.

I was in Missoula, Montana, recently, doing book promotion, when a young woman I had never met asked me out for coffee. A beloved editor we knew in common had passed away, and the idea was that we would get together and tell a few "Carol" stories.

"I have to admit," she said, when we had settled into our table, "that you and Terry Tempest Williams are my biggest literary heroes, and one thing I have always admired about you is that you are both childless by choice."

I realized when she said it how long it had been since anyone had found that particular aspect of my life admirable. What most people—especially women—found it, almost without exception, was selfish, misguided, or even mildly creepy, like the way Winona Ryder got away, at first, with shoplifting, but eventually, inevitably, got caught.

"What I want more than anything is to have a life like yours," she said, "writing, traveling, publishing books."

I knew she had recently sold her first book to a very good press and said, "It sounds like you are well on your way."

"The only thing is," she said, "I'm eleven weeks pregnant, and I guess why I really asked you out for coffee is that I was hoping you would tell me that I can have it all."

There it was again, that advertising slogan. While I stalled for time by sipping my latte, she told me she had similarly asked Terry out to coffee and presented her with the same conundrum. Kind, unsarcastic Terry, who had the benefit of being raised in a culture that values politeness so much more than we did back in New Jersey. However poorly she had scored on this unexpected test, she would have done a million times better than I.

Not to mention the tricky fact of eleven weeks, which was a lot different from four and also different from thirteen. Did this young woman *really* want me to tell her she could have it all, or did she want me to say, *Quick! Here's my cell phone. Make the appointment while there's still time!*

"How many weeks pregnant were you when you talked to Terry?" I asked, still stalling. When she looked at me strangely, I said, "I'm sorry. I guess I don't believe you *can* have it all. I don't believe any of us can. In fact, I believe the very expression *having it all* is not only a myth but also a symptom of how sick we are in our contemporary culture. Nobody gets to have it all, not even Donald Trump. You will have one thing or another depending on what choice you make. Or you will have both things in limited amounts, and that might turn out to be perfect, just exactly the life you want."

Feminist friends my age groan in agony when they meet young women who don't even know precisely what the words *Roe v. Wade* refer to. But, in fairness, what did I know, at eighteen, about Margaret Sanger, or everything it took to pass the Nineteenth Amendment, or how many states failed to ratify the ERA? Not nearly as much as I should have. Not enough to understand the debt of gratitude I owed to the women who had come before me.

But what is perhaps even more unsettling is my dawning understanding that because I came of age right on the heels of *Roe v. Wade*, of Gloria Steinem and Adrienne Rich, of Joan Didion and Alice Munro, it might have been more okay for *me* not to have children than it is for the women I met at Butler University. Maybe my generation had the distinct advantage of watching our own mothers see on the horizon the choices that would soon be available to women, only to realize how half buried they already were in the quicksand of overbearing husbands and carpool commitments and the Junior League. Maybe because we watched them retreat into the bottle, or the prescription pills, or worse, it was my generation who swore upon our Barbies and our Mystery Date board games that we would not be similarly trapped. Maybe those battles have fallen now, too far into the rearview mirror, or maybe, as Nan Nowik would say, the dominant paradigm has taught this generation of young women how to police themselves.

The first time I got pregnant was exactly nine months before my first book was slated to come out. I was twenty-nine years old, and I conceived around a diaphragm (with spermicidal jelly). The father of the child and I were not married, but we were in a decent enough relationship. I liked him a lot, which I understand now is probably the best thing one can say about any relationship, and I thought he would make a pretty good dad.

When I called to tell my mother I was pregnant, she said, "You have a very special talent, Pam, and if you decide to have that baby, you are going to become perfectly ordinary, exactly like everyone else." My mother was an actress, a singer, a dancer, and an acrobat. When she was sixty-five years old, she could still do handsprings down the beach. To cope with her life's disappointments, she drank three fifths of vodka per week and took a mountain of daily Vioxx, the combination of which would kill her within that year.

When I called my editor to tell *her* the news, she said

something much less pointed, though along the same lines and undeniably true. The publisher was behind my book of short stories in a way that was not so common—they were sending me on a multicity book tour—and it would be in the book's best interest if I was able to go.

Contrary to the belief of some outspoken congressmen, no woman ever *wants* to have an abortion. I have never met one who takes it lightly, who hasn't thought about the abortion with if not some version of regret, at least with some sadness for the rest of her life.

I have often wondered what would have happened if my mother had had a more standard reaction, for instance excitement about being a grandparent or a guarded hope that if I had a child, it might settle me down. Had there been even the slightest parental pause, space that would have allowed me to say how *I* was feeling about it, would I have made a different decision? Twenty-nine feels so young to me now—surely I thought I had unlimited time ahead of me. I was so naive about the pressures of the publishing industry I might have believed that if having the baby hurt this book's sales, I'd be given the chance to write and promote another. Had this all happened before *Roe v. Wade*, every single thing about my life right now would be different. Not necessarily worse and not necessarily better. I don't believe under any circumstances I would think I had it all.

I will admit without hesitation that my life is rich and full of pleasure. I love to work hard and I do, at both teaching and writing. When I'm teaching, my job is to make and hold a space for someone else's creativity; when I'm writing, I get to prioritize my own. I spend the money I earn at both pursuits on adventures that will lead to more writing, the publication of which will lead to better teaching opportunities, which will lead to more adventures, which will lead to more writing, and so on, if I am lucky, for the rest of my life. I value my time because it gives me the capacity to earn money and I value the money I earn because it buys me freedom, and these seem like reasonable priorities. I live on a spectacular piece of land in a spectacular part of Colorado. I paid off the mortgage last summer, after twenty-one years, with every single dime of the money I earned either teaching or writing. It feels to me, all in all, like a comparatively honorable life.

It also seems honorable that another woman would value motherhood over all my priorities. But I do not believe that I am selfish and she is not. There are women who choose motherhood for selfish reasons. There are mothers who act selfishly even if they chose motherhood in a burst of altruistic love. Selfishness and generosity are not relegated to particular life choices, and if generosity is a worthy life goal—and I believe it is—perhaps our task is to choose the path that for us creates its best opportunity. It is quite possible that I would be a less generous teacher, a less supportive partner, a less available friend if I had children of my own to take care of. Love is not a pie, the saying goes, but it is also true that there are only so many hours in a day.

Or, in the parlance of the Butler creative writers, is it necessarily a bad thing when a woman gets to be *all about herself*? Is that not what our feminist foremothers were trying to tell us, that if a woman actually had five minutes to be *all about herself* she might find a cure for breast cancer, or win an Olympic gold medal, or negotiate peace in Gaza, or become president of the United States?

A student sent me an e-mail telling me she was dropping out of my private writing group: "I love the group and will really miss it," she wrote, "but I can't see spending the money I ought to be spending on my children's education on my own." I pictured her imagining, as she wrote the e-mail, a bunch of women standing around giant pieces of brightly colored plastic playground equipment in the town where she lives nodding sagely at her sacrifice.

But what I wanted to ask was, *Why not? Why is their education more important, inherently, than yours? You are a very talented writer with immense potential. What if your children turn out, even after that expensive education, to be just a couple of dolts?*

The median home price in the town where she lives is $904,000, so we can rest assured that her kids are in no real danger of remaining uneducated. I do understand that it is noble to want what is best for one's children. But I worry that we have taken a big step backward if it is perceived as nobler still when doing for one's children comes at great expense to oneself.

My mother said one thing to me more than any other and it was "I gave up everything I loved for you." It was an expression she used for almost any occasion: to make me clean my room, to make me part my hair on the side, to make me wear my retainer, to make me sign on to one of her psycho diets, to make me wear those awful Ann Taylor jackets with the four-inch shoulder pads, to make me break up with whatever boyfriend. I could fill pages with the things this simple set of words had the power to make me do. Years after my mother died, my therapist asked me to make a list of the things my mother loved, and as usual I obliged him: acting, singing, dancing, tennis, sewing, travel, vodka.

"And how many of those things did she enjoy after you were born?" he asked me.

"All of them," I said. "Every single one of them, right up to her death."

"How about that?" he said. "Turns out the only thing she gave up was . . . what?"

"The condition of childlessness," I said, which I had to grant her is no small thing, and a condition I admit to loving myself.

And maybe it's love, unsurprisingly, that all this comes down to. And love, like selfishness and generosity, is not exclusive to one demographic; it infuses every single thing we do and are. I love the physical world and the experiences I get to have in it so deeply and completely that it threatens to break my heart every minute, and I have made countless life choices—

in addition to childlessness—to ensure that I can be out and in the world on my own terms almost all the time.

When I am puking my guts into a hole in the ground in Bhutan, I am loving the prayer flags that flutter over my head; I am loving my body's ability to preserve my life by expelling whatever poison I was too stupid *not* to consume; I am loving, in retrospect, the temple where I was given the cholera-tainted orange that has landed me in this position; and I am loving, most of all, the fact that some combination of luck, hard work, and skill has landed me on assignment in Bhutan, a place that has lived in my imagination since I was a map-devouring child. And for Bhutan, feel free to substitute Bolivia, Botswana, Laos, Serifos, Paris, Istanbul, or, while you're at it, Telluride, Provincetown, Grand Forks, or New Smyrna Beach, to name only the tiniest fraction of the totality of the places I love. And when I say I love them, I mean I love their particularities: the smell of the yak butter candles in the Gyantse monastery, the woman in Kasane with beads in her hair who took my hands and taught me to dance, the four gangly graduate students at the University of North Dakota who asked me, during my visit, if I wanted to get up at eight on Sunday morning to go to the gym and sit in a smelly little plexiglass box and watch them play basketball.

"When you look into your baby's eyes," my friend Sarah once said to me, "that will become your Tibet." I have no doubt that looking into one's own baby's eyes is many inexpressibly wonderful things, but one thing it is not is Tibet.

———

For the last seven years I have had the great and specific pleasure of being a stepparent, and I therefore have a somewhat more realistic idea about the amount of time and money and psychic energy a person commits to expending when she agrees to have a child. And when I say a *somewhat* more realistic idea, I mean exactly that. My stepdaughter was already six when I met her, and she lives with her mother most of the time. I love Kaeleigh with the kind of love that would make me throw myself in front of a freight train to save her, so along with some small idea of the sacrifice, I also have some small idea of the reward.

You might think the joy that loving Kaeleigh has brought into my life would make me regret my earlier decisions, but just the opposite is true. I believe my childlessness contributed to my ability to step unhesitatingly and fully into her life at a time when she really needed me. First, having Kaeleigh in my life was new and interesting (yes, Sarah, not unlike Tibet), and by the time it wasn't new anymore, I had fallen completely in love.

When I am at my best with Kaeleigh, I am able to show her a different type of life from the one her mother chose. In this house, I am the primary breadwinner and as such make most of the decisions; I fly 100,000 miles a year, sometimes to places she has never heard of. I took her to her first rock concert. I read her her first Salinger; I taught her how to ride a horse. On the other hand, I fly more than 100,000 miles a year, sometimes to places she has never heard of. I missed her eighth birthday celebration because I was stuck in O'Hare Airport, and I am almost never the one who holds her hair back when she gets sick.

I always used to say, when pressed about children, that I figured some kid would show up someday who needed something from me and I would be ready. Not only is that exactly what happened; it turned out I needed something she had to give, too. You might be tempted to say that with the arrival of Kaeleigh, I got to have my cake and subsequently eat it. You might even be tempted to say that now I have it all. But having it all is a slogan for ad execs and life coaches. I'll settle for having freedom of choice.

BEYOND *BEYOND MOTHERHOOD*

by

Jeanne Safer

Nobody will ever send me a Mother's Day card—one of those Crayola-decorated creations made by dedicated, not fully coordinated small hands. I will never search my newborn's face for signs of my khaki eyes, or my husband's aquamarine ones, or sing a lullaby. No child of mine will ever smile at me, or graduate, or marry, or dedicate a book to me. I will leave no heir when I die.

Now that infertility is so much in the news, this has become an increasingly familiar litany. But there is

a difference in my case: I chose this fate. I made a conscious
decision not to have a child.

I wrote these words in 1989, for a magazine article that would
eventually become my first book, *Beyond Motherhood: Choosing
a Life Without Children.* I was forty-two years old then,
married for nine years, a practicing psychoanalyst for fifteen,
and in the final stage of making the hardest, loneliest decision of my life—I waited till the bitter end of my fertile years
to commit myself—and I wept as I wrote them. When I saw
them in print, which made my assertions undeniably real, I
wept again.

Reading them now, twenty-five years later, at what I hope
is not the ripe old age of sixty-seven, I am still struck by their
stark power, the pain I was trying to work through by putting them down on paper and absorbing their impact. Of
course my original feelings came back, and I shed a few tears
of recognition and empathy with my younger self. But along
with that memory came a retrospective sense of pride and
gratitude at what I did and how I did it: I realize now that
this choice made my life possible.

It says something about the strength of the stigma, both
internal and cultural, besetting intentionally childless women
that I felt I had to publish this intensely personal explora-
tion (its subtitle was "A Therapist's Self-Analysis") under a
pseudonym. I even took the additional, totally irrational step
of insisting it be published in August, the traditional "shrinks'

month off," as if anyone who knew me and read it would know that I couldn't possibly have written it then because I wasn't in town. At the time I thought I was simply protecting my privacy, but now I see that my real motive for the subterfuge was to prevent the remote possibility that my patients, colleagues, and acquaintances would recognize me and judge me as harshly as I judged myself. Shame—for being selfish, unfeminine, or unable to nurture—is one of the hardest emotions to work through for women who are conflicted about having children. Of course, the small minority of women who decided against maternity early on may avoid the angst that engulfed me, because wanting a baby is irrelevant to their identity. The infertile, though they have anguish of their own, don't have the same struggle as I did because society assumes their hearts are in the right place, and does not question their femininity. At that time, I wasn't yet ready to stake my claim aloud.

Nor was I prepared for the flood of responses my confession elicited from readers. The magazine it appeared in, the excellent but short-lived *7 Days*, received more mail about the story than about anything else it had ever published. The topic had scarcely been written about before and it was clear that like-minded women felt that someone was speaking for them at last. Of course, the magazine also forwarded me a few letters from strangers asserting that I was misguided or neurotic, or both. Several were from helpful fellow therapists who recommended that I go back into analysis so that

I would come to my senses before it was too late. Entering this fray was, and still is, not for the faint of heart. But I knew I had to write a book about it.

Among the prospective nonmothers I knew as patients and as friends, one of the most momentous questions to be wrestled with was whether they would have regrets later on. Would their hearts and their homes feel too empty, too quiet? What would they have in common with their friends who were mothers? What kind of connection would they have to future generations? Would they feel fully feminine? How would they tolerate missing the less complicated gratifications of grandparenthood? To whom would they leave their stuff? These issues certainly tormented me. So as I spent the next several years expanding my article into a book, I tried to interview as many older women as I could. Of the fifty interviews I conducted, five were with women over sixty. These women offered a unique perspective. I needed to know if the passing decades made them question their decisions and what it was like to make such a radical decision in the days when women had little control over when they had babies, much less whether they had them at all. They had made their choices in the prefeminist days before reliable contraceptives were widely available, in a world where there was even less support than there is now for outliers like them. Each one was content with her life. They did not fear aging without progeny (many noted that having children was no guarantee of care), they were satisfied with their mates and themselves, and, quite strikingly, they were proud of their independent spirits.

In 1996, when the first wave of baby boomers turned fifty, I recounted the testimonies of some of my childless subjects for an op-ed in *The New York Times* and reported that none of those who had made a conscious choice was grief-stricken by reaching the end of the line; in fact, they expressed satisfaction with their decision and its consequences. In 2014, the last cohort of that generation—my generation—reached fifty. I have every hope that the intentionally childless among them will be just as much at peace with the path they took.

Nonmotherhood is forever. Making a conscious choice about something so fundamental, and so intertwined with one's own past, with society's expectations, and with notions of femininity and the purpose of life, takes every ounce of will you have; going against the grain always does. After the childbearing years pass, unless you opt to adopt or use a surrogate, you cannot reconsider. How did this critical decision, which of necessity I made intuitively, affect my destiny and sense of self? How, now that I am sixty-seven, does it continue to reverberate?

Revisiting the issue after a quarter century, I am relieved and delighted to report that I have never seriously questioned that the life I chose was right for me. In the five years it took me to come to my conclusion, I endured intense anxiety, self-doubt, sorrow, and a great deal of ambivalence about my future. But I realized in retrospect that most of that time was actually spent recognizing and accepting what I had already implicitly decided. The turning point came when, after seeing that I had run out of excuses and still wasn't enthusiastic about pregnancy or motherhood, I finally said to myself, "I don't really want to have a baby; I *want to* want to have a baby." I longed to feel like everybody else, but I had to face the fact that I did not. This meant that I had to work through the implications of being radically different from most other women in a fundamental way, that my requirements for happiness and fulfillment actually precluded the things they found crucial. I tried to confront every feeling I had, no matter how excruciating. Taking this route to self-fulfillment required that I pay attention to what I really felt, as opposed to what I was supposed to feel, or wished I did. Only then could I grieve for the lost possibilities that lay in all I was ruling out; grieving for the road not taken is a healthy thing to do. That has served me well.

I was also extremely lucky to have a husband who backed me up. He could have gone either way about having a family, but felt, realistically, that since motherhood was more all-encompassing than fatherhood, it ultimately had to be my decision. He made it clear that sharing his life with me was what mattered most to him. His attitude was one of the reasons I love him as I do. As a result, we have enjoyed a rare intellectual and emotional intimacy for the thirty-five years we have been married.

In the ensuing years, I have accepted that I might actually have made a better, or a happier or wiser, mother than I feared I would be. But I could not have predicted how much the things I merely suspected I needed turned out to be, in fact, exactly what I needed: freedom to do what I wanted, when I wanted (traveling the world, sleeping until noon, or going out to dinner or the movies at midnight on occasion); to concentrate on my relationship with my husband; to give myself completely to the dual careers of psychotherapy and writing. I realized that my initial instincts were right; I didn't want to be torn between my needs and those of another, particularly someone I had brought into the world. Trivial as it may sound, I'm thrilled I never had to set foot in Disneyland (or feel guilty about not taking someone there), or worry about playdates or, down the road, online pornography and all the other scourges of adolescence. I don't miss any of it. Neither do I feel selfish or "barren," as childless women used to be called (it is telling that there is no parallel term for childless men). Thanks to that conscious decision I made in early middle age, I can respond undefensively to the universal conversational gambit from strangers, "How many children do you have?," that embarrasses many childless women. "None," I say with a smile. "Motherhood was not for me."

The decision process itself has influenced me both personally and professionally in ways I couldn't have imagined, in ways beyond the issue of whether or not to become a mother. It led me to a stance I call the "Affirmative No." I define this stance as the refusal to pursue a course of action that, on serious reflection, you discover is not right for you.

Asserting an Affirmative No means rejecting attitudes

and courses of action (for example, always forgiving wrongs, or reflexively following doctors' orders) that most people treat as gospel. It also often means saying yes to points of view that may be unpopular but are in fact authentically in line with your own thoughts and feelings. Such conclusions are reached only through relentless self-awareness. Any decision made in this way is not an act of rebellion; it is an act of willed self-assertion, of standing your ground on your own behalf.

Refusing to act against your sound inclination is a profound *action*, not simply a reaction to something external. And to claim the benefits that come from advocating for the person you truly are as opposed to the one you think you're supposed to be, you must face your own reality no matter how it feels or what its implications may be.

The Affirmative No is the basis of authentic individualism. It has become the foundation of my philosophy of life and the cornerstone of my work with patients. It has inspired me to articulate the against-the-grain positions on the "taboo topics" that I have championed in all five of my books; it has also helped me preserve my identity through two serious illnesses. *Beyond Motherhood* paved the way.

So how does a woman who has chosen not to have children relate to a world that is full of them? I will probably never be as important to anybody—even my patients—as every mother is to her offspring. I gave up precious experiences and relationships so that I could have others that I needed even more. But I have found my own ways to be important to the next generation. Some women who made the same choice I did delight in being aunts to their siblings' children, or special adults in the lives of their friends' children, neither of which I have had the opportunity to do, but such roles might have suited me. In general, though, I have never been comfortable around young children, with the exception of a memorable seven-year-old girl whom I connected with when I worked in a children's psychiatric hospital in college. To be a model, mentor, and teacher of younger people in my field is a source of gratification for me. I especially enjoy working in therapy with young women, helping to set them up for a life of self-awareness and self-expression. I am glad that being childless has not prevented me from helping many women make decisions—in both directions—about motherhood, or from empathizing with mothers. I love the children of my patients from afar, and I feel deep satisfaction that I can give their parents good counsel about how to understand them.

When I reread my teenage diaries recently in preparation for a book project, I came upon a startling fact: I actually had begun to consider a voluntarily childless life in 1963, at age sixteen, when I wrote, "I've decided to live my life disproving that women's only creativity is bearing children." I didn't remember writing this, but my prophecy came true. I knew even then, well before I had to confront it. I just didn't remember that I knew.

When *Beyond Motherhood* was published, I was worried that my mother, whom I identified with in most other ways, would feel spurned and repudiated by the book that proclaimed my decision, and analyzed her role in it. Instead she was overjoyed. She had always, it turned out, wanted me to be a writer more than she wanted me to be a mother, and her pride was boundless. As much as I'd always felt she had oppressed me with her own needs, I realized then that she'd done even more to encourage my independence of mind. The book is dedicated to her.

How has the landscape changed for women who are childless by choice in the quarter century since I joined their ranks? Their numbers have increased—the percentage of women who opted out of maternity hovered around 10 percent of women of childbearing age when I wrote about it; now the number is rising, and they are more honest, more outspoken, and less apologetic and defensive—at least publicly. But I don't imagine human nature has changed dramatically; private anguish persists, as I discover from patients who come to me to help resolve their motherhood dilemmas. Most of them have discussed it with nobody and are plagued by the same distress and unanswered questions I remember so vividly. If you haven't rejected the possibility in advance, or embraced it automatically, you have to do the hard work of figuring out where you stand, and why. It is never easy.

Some things are definitely different—for both good and ill. In August 2013, *Time* magazine ran a cover story on the topic of deliberate childlessness, a first for them. The title was "The Childfree Life: When Having It All Means Not Having Children," and it was illustrated with a photograph of a glamorous, sexy, smiling (heterosexual) couple in bathing suits lying on the sand, unencumbered. I was glad that the subject was finally getting attention. Back in 1996, an editor at *Time*, who was childless by choice herself, interviewed me about *Beyond Motherhood*. But her supervising editor killed the story because he apparently could not accept my depiction of nonmothers as fruitful and feminine. He believed no woman could, or should, feel good about such a life. To my recollection, the magazine didn't cover the phenomenon again until 2013.

But while I was pleased to see the story, I was perturbed by the message, and by upbeat catchphrases like "having it all" and "childfree," which seemed to imply that denying a loss makes it disappear, or that acknowledging it means one feels incomplete. "These women," the author cheerfully asserted, "are inventing a new female archetype, one for whom having it all doesn't mean having a baby."

The problem is that there is nobody alive who is not lacking anything—no mother, no nonmother, no man. The perfect life does not and never will exist, and to assert otherwise perpetuates a pernicious fantasy: that it's possible to live without regrets. There is no life without regrets. Every important choice has its benefits and its deficits, whether or not people admit it or even recognize the fact: no mother has the radical, lifelong freedom that is essential for my happiness. I will never know the intimacy with, or have the impact on, a child that a mother has. Losses, including the loss of future possibilities, are inevitable in life; nobody has it all.

A thoughtful mother I know, who put her law career on hiatus to raise two sons, captured that truth in a note she sent me after she read my book: "I think of you often—your travels to exotic countries, your professional pursuits: in short, your adult life. Suburban motherhood is wonderful in many respects; there are moments so golden that they take my breath away. This is, however, also an extremely circumscribed existence. Not surprisingly, part of me craves your life."

Real self-acceptance, real liberation, involves acknowledging limitations, not grandiosely denying them. It is true, and should be recognized, that women can be fulfilled with or without children, that you can most definitely have enough without having everything. How fortunate we are to live in an era when we can make deeply considered choices about which life suits us, and that now the world looks slightly less askance if we go against the flow. Making the less common choice has its gratifications but also its drawbacks. Having enough—and having the right stuff for us—is all we can get, and all we need. For me, what I hoped in 1989 that I could achieve has come to fruition: my womb has always been empty, but my life is full.

OVER AND OUT

by

Geoff Dyer

I'VE HAD ONLY two ambitions in life: to put on weight (it's not going to happen) and never to have children (which, so far, I've achieved). It's not just that I've never *wanted* to have children. I've always wanted to *not* have them. Actually, even that doesn't go far enough. In a park, looking at smiling mothers and fathers strolling along with their adorable toddlers, I react like the pope confronted with a couple of gay men walking hand in hand: Where does it come from, this unnatural desire (to have children)? It comes, I suppose, from wanting to have sex. During the early 1970s, when I first became theoretically interested in sex, there was a considerable body of evidence to suggest that unless you were extremely careful, having sex could lead to unwanted pregnancy. Teen pregnancy was a bad thing, to be avoided through various "precautions" (a word that seemed deliberately chosen for its anti-aphrodisiac qualities). Maybe those early sex-education classes worked on me more powerfully than I realized: I'm fifty-six now and am still convinced that if I fathered a child it would be a belated instance of teen pregnancy.

I may be immune to but I am not unaware of—how could I be?—the immense, unrelenting, and all-pervasive pressure to have children. To be middle-aged and childless is to elicit one of two responses. The first: pity because you are *unable* to have kids. This is fine by me. I'm always on the lookout for pity, will accept it from anyone or, if no one's around, from myself. I crave pity the way other men crave admiration or respect. So if my wife and I are asked if we have kids, one of us will reply, "No, we've not been blessed with children." We do it totally deadpan, shaking our heads wistfully, looking as forlorn as a couple of empty beer glasses. One day I might even squeeze out a tear as I say it, but I haven't had the nerve yet. It's a touchy subject. People are surprisingly sensitive about these things.

The second: horror because by *choosing* not to have children, you are declining full membership in the human race. By a wicked paradox, an absolute lack of interest in children attracts the opprobrium normally reserved for pedophiles. Man, you should have seen what happened a couple of years ago when a friend and I were playing tennis in Highbury Fields, London, next to the children's area where kids were cavorting around under the happily watchful eyes of their mums. It's quite a large area, but it is, needless to say, not big enough. A number of children kept coming over to the tennis courts, rattling on the gate, and trying to get in. The watching middle-class mums did nothing to restrain them. Eventually my friend yelled, "Go AWAY!" Whereupon the watching mums *did* do something. A mob of them descended on us as though my friend had exposed himself. Suddenly we were in the midst of a maternal zombie film. It was the nearest I've ever come to getting lynched—they were after my friend rather than me and though, strictly speaking, I was his opponent, I was a tacit accomplice—and a clear demonstration that the rights of parents and their children to do whatever they please have priority over everyone else's. "A child is the very devil," wrote Virginia Woolf in a letter, "calling out, as I believe, all the worst and least explicable passions of the parents." Certainly at that moment, the threatened love these mums felt for their children seemed ferocious and vile, either a kind of insanity or, at the very least, a form of deeply antisocial behavior. I stress this because it's often claimed that having kids makes people more conscious of the kind of world they're creating or leaving for their offspring. That would be why, in London, a city with excellent public transportation, parents have to make sure they have cars. Many of these cars come speeding along my street on their way to the extremely expensive private school on the corner. You can see, from the looks on these mums' faces as they drop off their kids at this little nest of privilege, that the larger world—as represented by me, some loser on his bike—doesn't exist, is no more than an impediment to finding a parking

space. Parenthood, far from enlarging one's worldview, results in an appalling form of myopia. Hence André Gide's
verdict on families, "those misers of love."

There's something particularly abhorrent, by the way,
about that little school on my street. As I was walking past
one day—i.e., skulking by like a fucking nonce—I saw an
almost unbelievable sight: members of staff holding open the
doors of cars for these kids so that at the age of seven they
could start developing the sense of being visiting dignitar-
ies. Another time I offered a shopping bag full of used tennis balls to a kid on his way there; he declined as though he
were the aristocratic offspring of John McEnroe. To be presented with anything other than an unopened tube of
tournament-standard Slazengers was clearly a polluting experience for this little English Brahmin. In the interest of fairness, I'm happy to report that they were gratefully received
by the teachers and kids at one of the state schools around
the corner.

What these episodes make clear is that my feelings about
kids are inseparable from deep-rooted class antagonism. I
sometimes wonder if my aversion to having kids is because
if I did have one he or she would be middle-class, with all
the attendant expectations: the kind of child on whose behalf I'd make calls to friends at *The Guardian* or Faber and
Faber about a possible internship after he or she had graduated from Oxford or Cambridge. It's actually rather vile, the
nice part of London where I live. You can see the batons of

privilege, entitlement, and power being passed smoothly on from one generation to the next.

For many people, having and raising a child is the most fulfilling thing in their lives. Quite a few friends who'd been indifferent to having kids found that once the plunge had been taken, often accidentally, their lives had a meaning and purpose that they previously lacked. People realize that a life that had seemed enjoyable (travel, social life, romance) and fulfilling (work) was actually empty and meaningless. So they urge you to join the child-rearing party: they want you to share the riches, the pleasures, the joys. Or so they claim. I suspect that they just want to share and spread the misery. (The knowledge that someone is at liberty or has escaped makes the pain of incarceration doubly hard to bear.) Of all the arguments for having children, the suggestion that it gives life "meaning" is the one to which I am most hostile—apart from all the others. The assumption that life *needs* a meaning or purpose! I'm totally cool with the idea of life being utterly meaningless and devoid of purpose. It would be a lot less fun if it did have a purpose—then we would all be obliged (and foolish not) to pursue that purpose.

Okay, if you can't handle the emptiness of life, fine: have kids, fill the void. But some of us are quite happy in the void, thank you, and have no desire to have it filled. Let's be clear on this score. I'm not claiming that I don't need to have kids because my so-called work is fulfilling and gives my life meaning. To be honest, I'm slightly suspicious of the idea of an anthology of *writers* writing about not having kids. Obviously any anthology of writing is, by definition, full of stuff by writers, but if this is a club whose members feel they have had to sacrifice the joys of family life for the higher vocation and fulfillment of writing, then I don't want to be part of it. Any exultation of the writing life is as abhorrent to me as the exultation of family life. Writing just passes the time and, like any kind of work, brings in money. If you want to make sure I never read a line you've written, tell me about the sacrifices you've made in order to get those lines written. If we were able to go through history and eliminate every single instance of sacrifice, the world would be a significantly better place, with a consistently increased supply of lamb. Sacrifice is part of the parent's vocabulary, as Isaac discovered when Abraham pressed the knife to his throat, though it usually works the other way around, with parents sacrificing themselves for the greater good of their children. I was about to start ranting on about this when I remembered that I'd ranted on about it years ago in my book *Out of Sheer Rage*, the writing of which involved sacrifice on such an epic psychological and financial scale that I hope I'll be forgiven for quoting from it here:

> *Life for people with children is crammed with obligations and duties to be fulfilled. Nothing is done for pleasure. The child becomes a source of restrictive obligation. Even the desire to have children is expressed in terms of fulfilling a biological duty. The lies people lead!*

The perfect life, the perfect lie . . . is one which prevents you from doing that which you would ideally have done (painted, say, or written unpublishable poetry) but which, in fact, you have no wish to do. People need to feel that they have been thwarted by circumstances *from pursuing the life which, had they led it, they would not have wanted; whereas the life they really want is precisely a compound of all those thwarting circumstances. It is a very elaborate, extremely simple procedure, arranging this web of self-deceit: contriving to convince yourself that you were prevented from doing what you wanted. Most people don't want what they want: people want to be prevented, restricted. The hamster not only loves his cage, he'd be lost without it. That's why children are so convenient: you have children because you're struggling to get by as an artist— which is actually what being an artist means—or failing to get on with your career. Then you can persuade yourself that your children prevented you from having this career that had never looked like working out. So it goes on: things are always forsaken in the name of an obligation to someone else, never as a failing, a falling short of yourself. Before you know it desire has atrophied to the degree that it can only make itself apparent by passing itself off as an obligation. After a couple of years of parenthood people become incapable of saying what they want to do in terms of what they want to do. Their preferences can only be articulated in terms of a hierarchy of obligations—even though it is by fulfilling these obligations (visiting in-laws, being forced to stay in and baby-sit) that they scale the summit of their desires.*

A decade and a half later, I don't see any need to change this substantively, though I would perhaps change the tone to make it less forgiving, more vehement. Especially since I no longer mind missing out on the things that having kids might have prevented me from doing, like going to discotheques, which I used to enjoy enormously when I was sixteen, even though I pretty much hated every minute I spent in every disco I ever set foot in. All I really want to do these days is sit around feeling sorry for myself, and it's not like having a kid would interfere with that, unless extreme tiredness is some kind of antidote to self-pity. Parents are always saying how tired they are, and I believe them; I'm sure they are, even though I find it hard to believe that anyone could feel as tired as I do. I'm tired all the time, absolutely exhausted, from the time I wake up to the time I flop into bed a couple of hours later for the first of the day's reviving naps. Over the years these naps have lost their capacity to revitalize, in fact have lost their capacity to do anything except increase the need for more naps. There might be a moral here—there is in most things—but I'm too tired to work out what it is.

Going back to the missed-disco opportunities or forgone pleasures argument, this would be entirely valid if we were discussing the reasons I've never had a dog. Whereas it's never even occurred to me to have a *child*, I would love to have a *dog* but am put off by the burden of responsibility involved.

And while not having a child is a source of pleasure, not having a dog is a source of constant torment and endless anxiety for my wife and me. We keep wishing that we could arrange our lives in such a way that it was possible to have a dog, but we keep coming up empty-handed, empty-pawed.

Does this mean, as parents might claim, that I'm just too selfish? Now, there's a red herring if ever there was one. Not having children is seen as supremely selfish, as though the people having children were selflessly sacrificing themselves in a valiant attempt to ensure the survival of our endangered species and fill up this vast and underpopulated island of ours. People raise kids because they *want to*, but they always emphasize how hard it is. "You think it's hard bringing up children?" asked the comedian David Cross. "No. Persuading your girlfriend to have her third consecutive abortion, *that's* hard." It was a joke greeted with shrieks of laughter and horror. "I call that joke the Divider," he conceded once the howls had died down.

The other move put on you by the parenting lobby is that you should have kids because you might regret not doing so when you get older. This seems demented and irrelevant in equal measure since while life may not have a purpose, it certainly has consequences, one of which is the accumulation of a vast, coastal shelf of uncut, 100-percent-pure regret. And this will happen whether you have no kids, one kid, or a dozen. When it comes to regret, everyone's a winner! It's the jackpot you are guaranteed to win. I think I was about fourteen when I was obliged to swallow my first substantial helping of regret. I would like to claim that it was also my last, but it turned out to be the opening course of a never-ending feast. If I've never forgotten the taste, that is because under- or overcooked regret is the main dish—the very taste—of adulthood.

So if it was argued that the inability to take responsibility for a dog, together with a refusal to contemplate having children, was a symptom of severely arrested development, of unduly prolonged adolescence, I would agree—and disagree—wholeheartedly. Certainly I am yet to hear a convincing argument as to why I should spend more than about twelve hours a year, max, doing anything I don't want to do. Is that adolescent? Maybe. But it's a form of adolescence that is compatible with a highly developed, entirely un-adolescent sense of civic responsibility. I *am* a good citizen (look at the trouble I went to recycling those tennis balls) and a reliable, trustworthy friend. I just don't ever want to hear someone address me as *Daddy*, don't want to live in a house littered with brightly colored toys, don't want to stand on the opposite side of a tennis net patting the ball to an eight-year-old and saying, "Great shot!" on those rare occasions that he manages to tap it back. Of course if I'd had a kid sixteen years ago and forked out thousands of pounds for him or her to have tennis lessons—like every other privileged brat in the neighborhood—I might now have a perfectly compatible homegrown tennis partner, might not be reduced to lurking around the courts on Saint Mark's Road like a fucking nonce again, hoping somebody else might be cruising for a partner. Instead, I'm fifty-six and still living like I did when I was fourteen, without brothers and sisters, constantly on the lookout for someone to play tennis with.

It seems we've accidentally stumbled onto or into the heart of the matter. I'm sure that I would not be so averse to having children or so reluctant to take custody of a dog if I'd grown up with brothers and sisters or a pet. But it wasn't like that; it was just the three of us, just me, my mum, and my dog-hating dad. And now there's just me and my wife. If there'd been a moment when the urge to have a kid might have manifested itself, that would surely have been in 2011, when both of my parents died. The world reeled and yawed that year and eventually righted itself again. My wife is forty-seven. Her parents are still alive; her sister is forty-nine, single, and childless. So when we die, that's it for both sides of the family. The immense and complicated lineage, stretching back however long, with all its struggles and setbacks, victories and defeats, joys and pains, births and deaths, quarrels and reconciliations—all of this will come to an end with us. Within thirty or forty years, that will be that. Over and out, forever. The end of history, in a way. If there is such a thing as oblivion, then I've got a perfect view of how it might look and feel.

YOU'D BE SUCH A GOOD MOTHER, IF ONLY YOU WEREN'T YOU

by

M. G. Lord

WHEN MY MOTHER DIED, I stopped seeing in color. I was fourteen years old and afraid to tell anyone. Our lawn, which had never been particularly emerald, became gray-white. Our modest postwar house, once mustard, was now bleached sepia. Our ancient Dodge Dart, which actually was white, remained so—but its glacier-blue interior looked ashen. I memorized the one detail without which I could not survive: red was at the top of the light; green was at the bottom.

Suspecting a neurological problem, I feared I might have to go to the hospital, which was out of the question. We were broke. My mother had entered Long Beach Memorial Medical Center in Long Beach, California, in March 1970. Her doctors had not expected her to survive until April. But she lasted until Labor Day. My father's insurance did not cover this length of stay. Oppressed by the bills that arrived after her death, he was forced to sell the one object he and my mother had most cherished: their house in La Jolla. The house where I, their only living child, had been born five weeks prematurely on the kitchen floor. The house under whose avocado trees I was photographed in a sailor-themed hat at Easter and in a red stocking cap at Christmas. The house we'd had to leave when my father lost his aerospace job in San Diego and found another one near Los Angeles.

In a rented house, the colorless one, I learned the dark side of mothering—caring for the sixty-five-year-old toddler who was my father. He had designed the flight controls for the HL-10, one of NASA's first lifting bodies, a precursor to the space shuttle. But he claimed not to understand the controls on the washing machine. Or, for that matter, on the stove, vacuum, and steam iron. Not to mention the basic principle of the hamper. He dropped his socks and shirts on the floor wherever he removed them. I honestly don't think he did this to torture me. For his entire life, some woman—his mother, my mother—had picked up after him. They had cooked for him. He had no clue that another way was possible. We couldn't afford a housekeeper. After one of my inept meals—some components were burned; others sickeningly undercooked—I asked him why he never even tried to throw together a dinner. "Men don't do that," he said.

A teenager focused on quick solutions might have become a heroin addict. But I plotted. I had greater aspirations than housekeeping and adult-infant care. And my mother had had greater aspirations for me; I knew she had secured a savings account for college that my father couldn't access. Somehow I found time to edit the school newspaper, serve as senior class president, weather exhausting swim-team workouts, generate endless homework, and get myself into Yale, which, miraculously, was three thousand miles away from Long Beach.

This admission changed my life. In the 1970s, many people viewed New Haven as an emblem of urban blight: crumbling, crime-filled, edged by brutal public housing. But to me it was a Technicolor wonderland. I remember the postcard blue behind the tawny masonry of Harkness Tower. I remember the bottle-green grass on the Old Campus, the verdigris lions guarding Wright Hall, the scarlet foliage that burst out everywhere in October. I remember the frail orange light inside the marble walls of my favorite structure, the Beinecke Library.

For the first time since my mother's cancer diagnosis, I saw rainbows—in their full, giddy, ROYGBIV splendor. Each day, I worked hard, astonished that I did not have to plan meals, do other people's laundry, or scrub the bathroom floor. On the university health plan, I saw a therapist for the first time—as well as a neurologist and an ophthalmologist.

We discussed my sight. They found no physiological problems. Acute depression, the therapist speculated, may have caused my plunge into black and white.

My color vision remained intact for more than thirty-five years, some of which were bumpy. They included professional false starts, a fourteen-year marriage, a divorce, and a breast lumpectomy. They included deciding after my divorce to date women, and conveying this confusing information to some less-than-welcoming friends and relatives. They included a move from New York to Los Angeles for work. But no pothole was so deep—no incident so traumatizing—that it robbed me of color. Until two years ago, when my then life partner unilaterally decided to adopt the fifth offspring of a twenty-two-year-old middle school dropout in Florida, a woman whose biological mother had herself died in her twenties of a drug overdose.

Eight years ago, when I met Helen, which is what I will call my former partner to protect her privacy, we clicked. Such clicking was not, for me, a frequent occurrence. She was smart, well educated, and droll enough to make me laugh. I was fifty; she was forty-one. I responded to a profile on an online site that she had planned to delete but somehow forgot. Its headline, as I recall, was "Soprano Seeks Mezzo." I think I signed my e-mail "Octavian," and she knew I was alluding to *Der Rosenkavalier*, my favorite opera. Having weathered many apocalyptically mismatched dates, I found this knowledge so stunning as to be a sign from God.

Helen had studied film, music, and art history. She had worked as a music editor for film and television. We obsessed over identical things. Well, almost identical. Even eight years ago, she dreamed that she would one day be someone's mother. I dreamed that I would one day win the Publishers Clearing House sweepstakes and a Nobel Prize. I was flippant about my "dream" and assumed she had been the same. But she wasn't. Three years ago, she became deadly serious. We were working closely as writing partners on several projects, but suddenly—and, for me, bafflingly—engaging work took a backseat to a new fixation: securing a human newborn.

Many women who lost their mothers as children go on to flourish as mothers themselves. Some claim to have healed their grief through parenting. I wanted to be one of those women. When the prospect of a baby loomed on my horizon, I felt pure horror. But I thought I could white-knuckle my way through this and become a different person, a better person. I pictured myself not so much as a co-parent but as a benign auntie, who would take care of Helen—making sure she ate and even occasionally slept—while she took primary care of a newborn. The simple acts of diaper changing and feeding might connect me with an infant; I would finally understand and feel an attachment that I didn't believe was possible. My body, however, was not onboard with this plan. It slowed me down. It gave me weekly eighteen-hour migraines.

Then it clobbered me with its nuclear weapon: loss of color vision. It gave me no choice. I had to look back at my past to discern why I could not move into the future.

Even as a child, I never wanted to nurture. I hated baby dolls, but not nearly as much as I hated actual babies. They stank, yowled, and interfered with my greatest pleasure: reading. In elementary school, my mother helped me memorize multiplication tables and write book reports. She had, for reasons she never made clear, dropped out of graduate school in chemistry. But she loved to explain science. When she squeezed fresh orange juice, she pointed out the molecular difference between ascorbic acid (in citrus) and acetylsalicylic (in aspirin), molding me into the pedant that I am today. She co-led our Brownie troop, and held me hostage in the backyard for a week while she taught me to hit a baseball. She was a natural athlete, a good tennis player, and her daughter would not be the last chosen for a team. (I became the second-to-last.) For all these gestures, and for just paying attention, I loved my mother. I know I survived my difficult years, the years after she was gone, because I had once felt so deeply loved by her.

At home, she toed the party line: "The greatest calling for a woman is to be a Catholic wife and mother." But I sensed that she hated the 1960s convention of stay-at-home motherhood. In my thirties, when my father shipped me my old Barbie-doll cases that had been sealed in storage since my mother's death, I found evidence of her unhappiness. My Barbie stuff was a mirror of her values. She never told me that marriage could be a trap, but she refused to buy my Barbie doll a wedding dress. She didn't say, "I loathe housework," but she refused to buy Barbie pots and pans. What she often said, however, was "Education is power." And in case I was too thick to grasp this, she bought graduation robes for Barbie, Ken, and Midge.

I also got the sense that giving birth was the worst hell imaginable. People say mothers "forget the pain," but mine didn't. It wasn't that she told people about her excruciating thirty-six-hour labor with my older sister, who was born with Down syndrome and died two weeks later. But she would recount my birth as a comic monologue in contrast to it. In November 1955, feeling what she thought might be labor, she rang her OB-GYN, who scoffed that I wasn't due for at least a month. Shortly thereafter, I plopped out on the kitchen linoleum. Our next-door neighbor ran to help. But at the sight of blood and amniotic fluid, the neighbor passed out. When the EMTs arrived, they found two women on the floor. "Which one do we take?" they asked. Nor did my mother convey that a child with developmental challenges—a child like my dead sister—was something to be sought out. My mother was not a social worker. "If the Lord sends you a trial," she told me, "you rise to meet it." But you'd have to be nuts to take on an unnecessary trial.

After her first surgery for colon cancer, when she was forty-nine years old, she took me with her to six o'clock Mass every morning. If anyone deserved a miracle, she did. And at age twelve, I enjoyed the liturgical component of the Mass:

so many idioms in common speech had their roots in the Old or New Testament. But three years and as many surgeries later, when her cancer proved fatal, I raged against God. This troubled her. To my amazement, she had not, apparently, lost her faith. On the day before she died, she told me to hold my ear close to her face. Her five-foot-ten-inch body now weighed about eighty pounds. She had tubes and bruises everywhere. She clutched a jade-green rosary in one gaunt hand and held mine with the other. "I love you," she rasped, barely able to form words through the morphine. I fought back tears. "God gave you gifts. Use them. And remember"—her weak voice became even softer—"God showed you one great mercy. He took your sister from us before you were born."

Because of my sister, I had no illusions about childbearing. It is a gamble, as is most of life. Money managers use the "Monte Carlo method" to evaluate portfolio risk—and to keep that risk within an investor's comfort zone. NASA never expects a risk-free launch, but it tries to fire rockets when they are less likely to blow up.

Similarly, when two educated, healthy young adults conceive a baby, the baby may have problems—even if the mother shuns drugs, alcohol, and nicotine during pregnancy. But the odds favor a healthy baby.

In contrast, I knew that the biological child of drug-addicted felons might be at a higher risk for problems. But given how badly my partner wanted a baby, any baby, I wanted to believe that nurture could defeat nature. If a child with no genetic advantages grew up in a loving, cultured home, the child would turn out well. This idea gave me comfort—until circumstances conspired to prove that it was not necessarily true.

Sometimes coincidences are so strange and pointed that it's hard to believe the universe is random. About a year after Helen began her quest to secure a baby, I agreed to be a judge for the National Book Award in Nonfiction. To do my job, I had to pore over stuff I otherwise would have avoided—books about recent breakthroughs in genomics and gestational biology, books that dwelled on the genetic determinants of behavior, books that examined the specific havoc drugs and alcohol can wreak on a fetus.

These books alerted me to things that I never wanted to see and, worse, that I couldn't put out of my mind. Cigarettes, I knew, were bad for pregnant women, but I'd had no idea how little nicotine was required to cause intellectual disabilities or aggressive behavior in kids. "If a mother smokes during pregnancy," neuroscientist and criminologist Adrian Raine writes in *The Anatomy of Violence: The Biological Roots of Crime*, this "not only has negative consequences on brain development, but it also leads to increased rates of conduct disorder and aggression in her offspring." (One has to wonder how many behavioral disorders were undiagnosed in, say, the 1960s, when smoking during pregnancy was less stigmatized than it is now.) He continues: "Studies have documented impairments in selective attention, memory, and speed in processing speech stimuli." More startling, "secondhand exposure to cigarette smoke predicted conduct disorder even after controlling for antisocial behavior in the parents, poor parenting practices, and other biological and social confounds."

Studies of identical twins raised in different environments—a loving, advantaged home versus a home with domestic abuse—revealed that the twins turned out the same. Their genes dictated who they were, not their upbringing. One Northern European study showed that not only did the home make no difference, but also that the children of criminals tended to grow up to be criminals. Raine's book and others like it gave me nightmares. In one recurring dream, I saw an illustration from *The Anatomy of Violence* that compared the MRI of a normal brain and the brain of a child with fetal alcohol syndrome. The normal brain had coils and whorls; the fetal-alcohol one looked like a cauliflower.

Still, I did not break up with my partner. I didn't want to be this fearful person, saddled with inconvenient knowledge that I could not banish from my thoughts. I didn't want to see the world as it was. I wanted to see it through a rosy, hopeful scrim. I loved having a partner; banal chores like cooking and shopping became adventures when done together. I loved watching great episodic TV with her—shows like *The Wire* and *House*—and analyzing how the TV writers had achieved what they did. I loved writing with her, in forms that were collaborative: a treatment, a script, a libretto for an opera that had a workshop production.

If only I had been twenty-five years younger! A quarter century ago, when I was married to my ex-husband, I had tried without success to bring a baby to term. A biological child made sense to me then—wanting to continue my genes, even if those genes carried depression so intense it could steal color from vision. But at my present age, with not that many productive years left, the last thing I wanted was a child—especially, I am ashamed to admit, one who might have disabilities as severe as those of my sister.

In the second decade of the twenty-first century, popular culture focused on nontraditional families—families with gay parents, or it-takes-a-village child-care arrangements with "families" of nonbiologically related adults. In response to my hesitation about adopting this baby—and the weekly migraines that accompanied it—my partner proposed that we devise such an arrangement. When the baby arrived, I could live in my "office" (a loft I owned) and escape baby duty from time to time. To defray the costs of a private adoption, she proposed teaming up with a close straight male friend who lived nearby and longed to be a dad.

In retrospect, I should have left the relationship. I should have heard my body's message. It knew who I was and how far I could travel from my core self without breaking. But my brain, or at least part of it, was intrigued to be part of a social experiment. My partner and the aspiring dad registered with an adoption lawyer and, after a few months, a birth mother on the west coast contacted them. The biological father of the potential baby was in prison, but we were prepared for this sort of news. My partner had warned me that it was not unusual in this situation for fathers to be incarcerated, or for mothers to be uncertain as to who the fathers were. In choosing my partner to raise her baby, this birth mother seemed both open-minded and admirable. Unlike many women in her situation, she had made it to her twenties without having had any babies and was enrolled in a community college. She was eager to take prenatal vitamins and to submit to drug and alcohol tests during her pregnancy. Because of her conscientiousness, I allowed myself the luxury of hope.

What happened next is what often happens. The mother decided to keep her baby. Because she was not a drug addict, she was hit hard by the oxytocin that her body released when she held her infant daughter. (For active drug addicts, oxytocin can't always compete with the pull of methamphetamine or heroin.) My partner was devastated—perhaps all three of us were. We had fleshed out a collective fantasy about making a "better" life for a kid, a life with love (from my partner) and financial advantages. We had to regroup.

Call me monstrous—and I'm sure some will—but after the disappointment, I was relieved that the mother had kept the baby. In the months that followed, the three of us rescued a dachshund-beagle mix, which mostly lived with the potential dad. To my shame, I hoped that dog would satisfy Helen's desire to nurture.

Then the twenty-two-year-old pregnant woman from

Florida entered the picture. Even my therapist, who tends to see good in all things, sensed danger. The woman had given birth to four kids since she had left school at age fourteen. And while she appeared to have kept one or two, some had been given up for adoption. In private adoptions, prospective parents agree to pay the mother's nonrefundable medical costs. But sometimes an illegal transfer of money also occurs, usually when the mother relinquishes the infant. Many people, I learned, refer to this illegal exchange as the "final shakedown." Although the woman was well along in her pregnancy, she had no prenatal records that might have revealed drug abuse. The lack of a paper trail can be a red flag for adopters. My partner paid for some basic medical tests. When the results came in, my partner texted me, "No HIV, no hep, no drugs"—at least at the time of the test. "Smokes, but main side effect of smoking is low birth weight and baby is normal."

The texts hit me like shots from an automatic weapon. I rolled into a fetal position on the bed. My partner knew well what I had discovered about nicotine and pregnancy. She knew everything that I (and science) knew about prenatal drug abuse. But she scoffed when I reminded her. She also knew what Hugh Laurie's character had said in nearly every episode of *House*: "Everybody lies." And addicts lie the most.

Some people are energized by risk. There's no reason why they shouldn't be. But in a relationship, the risk tolerance of partners should match. To draw upon the wisdom of Aesop, ants should not marry grasshoppers. I am an unglamorous ant—deferring gratification, socking away money religiously and investing it prudently. My partner was a grasshopper—seeking what she wants when she wants it, unconcerned by the threat of a rainy day.

I suspect that when she flew from Los Angeles to meet the pregnant woman, she was fueled as much by risk as by her urge to be a mother. Back home in my loft, I felt unheard and abandoned—because I was. I did not even log on to read e-mail. At dusk, I curled up on my bed, watching the light and color drain from my loft.

In the morning, when the sun came up, the color did not return.

One monochromatic week became two. I had kept the jade rosary my mother grasped at the hour of her death. Sometimes I held it when I sat cross-legged to meditate. It was now dark gray.

Strangely, I did not break up with my partner. I threw myself into work, spending most days with students or colleagues at the university where I teach. I told no one about the loss of color. But I couldn't keep the migraines entirely to myself. I had to explain why I sometimes missed a meeting. Blessedly, I never had to miss a class.

One night, after an evening class, I opened up to a colleague about what I was going through. We were sitting in a gastropub near campus. "I can't do it," I told him. "Not knowing what I now know from reading those books I never wanted to read." The anxiety—the risk—was causing migraines. With the first prospective child, at least I'd had the comfort of the birth mother's regular drug tests. That fetus, I knew, was not awash in bourbon and crystal meth. But this birth mother had no comprehensive medical records. The baby had no known father. The birth mother was herself the child of a woman who had died of a drug overdose. "I want to believe that nurture trumps nature," I said with desperation.

Instead of reassuring me, he told me a story—his story—that may not have been easy to tell. He is a brilliant gay man and an accomplished screenwriter who grew up in North Carolina. His childhood home was filled with books and music and art—all of which he devoured from a very young age. He has two older adopted siblings, however, who ignored these cultural resources. Nor were they good at or interested in school. Today they have both become what their biological parents were: uneducated members of a homophobic Christian cult. Because my colleague—their brother—is gay, they severed all ties to him. Then they cut off their adoptive parents, because the parents had the impunity not to disown a gay child.

This wasn't what I wanted to hear. But it was what I needed. In real life, nature could be as powerful—and as harsh—as it appeared to be in scientific literature.

No longer could I pretend to be in a relationship with someone who aggressively disregarded my informed opinion. I broke up with Helen. The headaches stopped. Again I saw in Technicolor.

As it happened, my now ex-partner did not get the infant

whose problematic provenance had caused our split. The mother decided to keep it, or perhaps ditched one prospective parent for another. Eventually, Helen adopted an infant from a different faraway state. I know little about this baby, except that she is a girl and her biological mother died in jail a month after giving birth. I learned this when, after I had not seen her for six months, my ex-partner invited me to retrieve a bike rack that I had left at her house. "How can I tell my daughter that her mother is in 'heaven' when I don't believe in heaven?" she asked.

I did not have to find an answer. God, as my mother might have observed, had spared me yet again.

Sometimes clichés are true. It does, for example, take a village to raise a child, and my role is to be a mentor. My students tell me that I'm good at this. Nor do I just teach graduate students at a private university. Last summer, I volunteered as a writing coach with high-achieving financially disadvantaged high school students. If they can do well against all odds—in homes where no one went to college and where English may not be spoken—they deserve my help. I also think our planet needs responsible stewardship—or there will be no planet for the kids growing up today. So I donate time and money to a marine mammal rescue center. Neither tutoring nor rescuing is a huge thing, but they make me feel less powerless against economic injustice and environmental destruction.

After I broke up with my partner, a friend told me something that was inadvertently cruel. "You would have been a great parent," she said, "if all those tragedies in your childhood hadn't happened." But they did. They made me who I am—not a hypothetical perfect person but a flawed mess, who is trying, however inadequately, to leave behind a better world than the one through which I have had to make my way.

THE HARDEST ART

by

Rosemary Mahoney

ONE DAY IN 2008 I was hiking up a mountain path in Greece when I met a farmer descending the path on a mule. The brim of his handwoven straw hat was unusually wide; in the broiling midday sun all but his feet and his hands on the reins were sheltered within a bell jar of shadow cast by the hat. The farmer, likely in his sixties, had Windex-blue eyes and a plush mustache the white of crushed ice. At its tips, left and right, the mustache swung jauntily upward into two little points. He was riding sidesaddle. From the opposite side of the saddle hung a large white sack.

The farmer looked surprised to see me there on this remote footpath. He stopped the mule and said good afternoon to me in the singular informal form. Because he was probably twenty years my senior, I said good afternoon in the

formal plural form. He considered me for a second, then began asking me the standard questions elderly Greek farmers
always ask: *Where are you going?*

To the church of Agios Nikolaos of the Air, at the top of
the mountain.

Where are you from?

The United States of America.

Flies waltzed noisily in the mule's left ear. *Are you alone?*

Do you see anyone else here on this path with me?

The farmer's sudden burst of laughter made the cylinder
of shadow jitter around him. *Are you married?*

Yes.

That was a lie, but in Greece, more than in any other country I've ever been to, marriage functions as a sanctified shroud
and shield.

Do you have children?

Usually, to save time and trouble, I would lie about this
one as well. But because I liked the farmer's face, I told the
truth: No, I do not have children.

He shrugged, raised his chestnut-brown hands toward the
overhanging sun, and with a surprisingly tender blend of pity,
sympathy, and resignation, he said, "Ότι θείλει Ο Θεός. Whatever God wants."

It would have been impossible for me to explain to him
that my not having children had nothing to do with what
God wanted and everything to do with what I wanted, for
in Greece (I might as easily say "for in the entire universe"),
a woman who doesn't want children is anomalous, aberrant,

and suspect. To choose not to have children is to stretch too far outside the inherited rule that procreation is both a biological and a civic requisite for full and proper membership in the human race. Conversations about this with elderly Greeks more often than not prove circuitous and fruitless, and so I lifted my own hands slightly to the sky and said, "Right. God's will." When I asked the farmer whether he had children, his answer was, surprisingly, no. His reason: *I never found a wife.*

Before we parted, I asked the farmer what was in the sack.

"Mizithra," he said. Goat cheese.

"Did you make it yourself?"

He grinned and the points of his mustache pricked at the jutting cheekbones above them. He waved his hands at the wheat fields and olive trees. "Do you see anyone else here who might have made it?"

We laughed and moved on.

My decision not to have children came at the end of a long, complicated, and sometimes fraught process of discovery that carried me as close to having children as a woman can possibly get. For most of my life I believed I would have children. When I was younger I used to imagine what my children would look like, and those pleasant imaginings made me love them so much that when I finally snapped to I would actually miss their faces. Even after embarking on a career as a writer, a job that consumed me with a lot of international travel followed by long bouts of work that left time for little else, I continued to think of my children as a certainty of my future. I never stopped to consider, though, how the certainty would become reality or how a person like me—solitary, over-sensitive, impatient, obsessive, easily abraded, and extreme—would manage to be a mother. It would, I thought, just work itself out.

Then, when I was thirty-seven, I read by chance some statistic about the drastic decline in fertility in women after age thirty-five and began to panic and fret about it. At that time I was living with a man I loved. We had never discussed having children and had in fact done everything in our power to keep from having them. When I raised the subject with him, he evaded it. He wasn't ready. He wasn't sure he ever wanted children. To placate me, he would say, "Soon," and after a few months he would still have decided nothing. Two years went by that way, and I realized that by dragging his feet he was passively asking me to choose between him and my chance of having children. He had a right to ask me to choose. What he didn't have a right to do was string me along and simply ignore the question. That felt extremely disrespectful to me. Finally one day I demanded a definitive answer, and when I got yet more avoidance and evasion, I slapped his face hard enough that my hand tingled. That was satisfying for about ten seconds, and then I felt like a pig. I, too, was respon-sible for this. I was so absorbed in my work that I had let the years go by without considering how I would actually get children or, far more important, what was really involved in raising them. "Soon" was as much my answer as his.

The man and I split up, which always takes longer than you think it will—the months of wavering and reversing, the fresh avowals that it's over, followed by periods of not com-municating, then the backsliding, the nights spent together that are better than any of the nights that went before, and finally the slow creep to knowing once and for all that it really is completely finished. Once we had finally split up, I knew that the chances of meeting someone else I could love who would also want children and want them in the same hurry that I was in were slim. I considered all the various ways a woman could have a child alone and finally, when I was forty, I went to an introductory meeting at a clinic in Boston that acted as an agency for various national sperm banks. I was the oldest woman in a room of eighteen women. Half of them were lesbians, many were single, and two of them were married to men with very low sperm counts. We were given an array of facts and statistics, as well as some very direct answers to our hesitant questions. Only 12 percent of women over forty become pregnant with frozen sperm. As women age, their eggs develop harder shells and sperm have more difficulty penetrating them. The oldest woman to become pregnant in the history of their program was forty-three, but that was a rare case. No, the donors were not home-less men who stumbled in off the street. The majority were graduate students putting themselves through school. Yes, the men were thoroughly screened for their personal, gene-tic, and health history, so really there was nothing to worry about.

I imagined them coming to donate sperm, those graduate students I was always seeing on the streets of Boston. The city was full of them—gangly MIT students with astrophysical pimples and unwashed bangs hanging damply over their thick-lensed eyeglasses, young men whose narrowly focused scientific genius rendered them socially imbecilic. Did I want one of them for the father of my kid? And money aside, what made these boys want to donate their sperm in the first place? How could they not feel awful about splashing out scores of kids they'd never know just for a couple of bucks? That, to my mind, was the biggest strike against them—the insouciance, the genetic profligacy, the carelessness.

Myself, I would not be able to give away even one of my children, let alone dozens. We learned that there was a limit to how many children a donor could legally generate. Twenty. There were states in which the sale of a donor's sperm was forbidden because he had already impregnated too many women in that area. Obviously the more anonymous children you have in one geographical region, the more likely it is that they'll meet in math class, fall in love, and enter unwittingly into a relationship. And all of that could happen without the biological father's ever knowing a thing about it.

As I've said, I am impatient. Colossally so. I sorely resented the tedious logistics of the artificial insemination process, the medical appointments that had to be made and endured, the registrations with the sperm banks, the choosing of the donor, the conferences and consultations, the blood tests, the four hundred dollars shelled out for a vial of sperm, which is probably the cheapest substance in the world and one that most men are happy to dispense for free, the three months of taking my temperature every morning to determine the exact date of ovulation, the waiting for the results. The whole thing was a mountain of impersonal, clinical complication. I loathed the thought of climbing it. Nevertheless, I wanted a chance. I felt that I couldn't go forward with my life without at least trying to bring my child into the world.

I began to study donors' profiles, handwritten answers to questions so detailed and in-depth that it could take half an hour to get through one of them. I learned the donors' height, weight, hair color, ethnicity, number of siblings, medical history, medical history of all known relatives, occupation, education, SAT scores, and more. Many of them surprised me with their honesty. There was the guy who admitted he'd had pubic lice, another who was married and had three children, another who was depressed after a traumatic event but was now "okay," the guy with the "mentally retarded" sister, the guy whose father died in the Spanish Civil War, another whose mother died in a hunting "accident," the one whose father had trouble with drugs, the one who had a brother who died four hours after birth, the one who had cancer, the one who had poor eyesight, the one who had been in prison for drunk driving when he was young, the one who was a security guard and clearly didn't know how to spell.

Some of the men interested me because of their family histories, others because of their own. The men who said that there had never been any problems of any kind in their lineage I didn't believe and rejected quickly. I preferred those who admitted to some drug use, poor eyesight, bad teeth, suicide, or a propensity for diabetes. Because I knew that the healthiest child comes from the widest mix of genes, I rejected the donors who were ethnically similar to me: all of the Irish, most of the English and Scottish, and a good number of the pale-skinned Northern Europeans. Because I knew that art was a terrible way to make a living, I leaned toward the scientists, the mathematicians, and those who had the highest level of education. I read their personal essays carefully. If the essay was no good, I put the whole file in the reject pile.

Eventually, I narrowed them down to one. A six-foot-tall blue-eyed Iranian American. He played the trumpet in some philharmonic orchestra near San Francisco, was getting a PhD in nuclear physics at Stanford, seemed to have a relatively healthy family history, and, best of all, his essay was well written, thoughtful, and witty. I bought a vial of his sperm, then wondered how I could guarantee that when the sperm was delivered at my door it was from the right donor. What if I ended up not with the Iranian sperm but with some Outer Mongolian sperm I hadn't asked for? (The four hundred dollars I paid for the sperm was nonrefundable, by the way.)

I loathed the whole process and went through it in a trance of blind obedience and baffled disbelief. It was surreal. Pregnancy was supposed to happen naturally, harmoniously, and without much effort, but here I was doing it in the most complicated way possible. And of course, since I had allowed myself to come this far, I was finally forced to think about how I would raise the child all by myself.

Philip Larkin averred that he disliked children because of "their noise, their nastiness, their boasting, their back-answers, their cruelty, their silliness." I, too, dislike these qualities in children. (Who doesn't?) Children can be wicked, insane, insufferable little shits. And yet I love them. I love them—especially the small ones—because of the way their emotions dance and glow on the surface for all to see. They have neither the guile nor the wile to hide how they feel. Very quickly, you know who they really are.

I love a child named Nat who's three and a half years old. When I show up at his house to visit his parents, he runs to the door and says, "Rose, may you play with me?" Usually I do. We stomp up the stairs to his parents' bedroom to watch *My Little Pony*, a TV show that is less thematically peculiar but more chromatically lurid than the Teletubbies. This particular show is about a pack of pastel-colored cartoon ponies with wings. They fly in a floating, hovering fashion, bobbing up and down in the drugged and dreamy way of merry-go-round horses. At Nat's request, I sit on the bed to watch. He stands close by me with a stuffed replica of one of these ponies clutched in his hand. He tells me her name is Princess

Celestia. She has hair the color and texture of cotton candy. Her body is encased in a shiny quilted fabric, like an astronaut's suit. Nat says, "She has a unicorn horn."

So she does. It's like the narrow end of a parsnip jutting out of her forehead. "Oh," I say, "she's a unicorn."

"No, she is a pony."

"But some of these ponies have a horn."

"*Yes*, Rose," he says, as though there's hope for me yet. "A unicorn horn."

"So, that makes them unicorns."

The smooth little face folds in displeasure. He steps toward me and gives me a brownish frown to show me I'm spoiling his evening with my obtuse incomprehension. "NO! They are *po*-nies!" His eyes seem to swell in his head in a way that suggests tears are imminent. Quickly I relent. "Okay, then. I get it. They are ponies with unicorn horns."

Soothed, Nat goes back to staring at the TV, mesmerized, transported. As the ponies sway over the poppies, he tells me their names: Twilight Sparkle, Rarity, Prince Blueblood. I begin to understand that those who have horns can't fly. "And that is Ribbon Wishes," Nat says. "Her brother is Somber Lightning. . . . "

It gets tired fast. There is only so much *My Little Pony* a reasonable adult can stand. After a respectable period of time, I stand up and suggest that we take Celestia downstairs and join Nat's parents in the kitchen. "No, Rose!" he shrieks, hopping up and down on the bed. "Don't leeeeeave! Watch *My Little Pony* with me!" He jumps to the floor, grabs my hand,

and leads me back to the bed, and when I sit again he puts an arm around my neck in what is part hug, part half nelson. He breathes on my nose. He is desperate to keep me here, desperate to share his interest with someone.

"Look, Rose, look! That's Sweetie Belle! See? Look, Rose! And Flim and Flam and Princess Luna and Sunset Shimmer and . . ."

The frantic geyser of chatter is calculated to hold me firmly in the room. It brings to mind a passage in literature that struck me with the force of its truth when I first read it. Exhausted after two weeks of minding his five-year-old son entirely by himself while his wife, Sophia, was away, Nathaniel Hawthorne wrote in his journal:

> The old boy is now riding on his rocking horse, and talking to me as fast as his tongue can go. Mercy on me, was ever a man before so be-pelted with a child's talk as I am! It is his great desire of sympathy that lies at the bottom of the great heap of his babblement. He wants to enrich all his enjoyments by steeping them in the heart of some friend.

Who could blame anyone, child or adult, for wanting to enrich his experience by sharing it with a friend, a caring witness? We all want that. We all want someone to say, "That thing you love is so interesting and worthy that I have to love it, too." Children's needs and desires are not so different from adults' needs and desires; the only real difference is that, unlike adults, children are not yet bridled. They haven't yet been forced to conform, to fit in, to behave. They haven't learned to be ashamed of their emotions, to repress their spontaneity, to hide their flamboyance and truth. They have not yet learned to navigate the world with the constant torpid pretense that they feel far less than they really do. They are inveterate liars and yet they are refreshingly truthful. When a five-year-old child comes into the classroom and says to his teacher, *Mrs. Smith, why is your face so flat?* the question is innocent, direct, and not entirely unreasonable. Smith's face *is* flat, and the boy wants to know why and hasn't yet been programmed to hide his curiosity and his true feelings about her notable and—to him—slightly disagreeable physiognomy. If Mrs. Smith is quick, she will say, *Well, Jimmy, we all have to accept the face we were born with*, and then, after a long pause during which she pointedly studies *his* face, she will add, *Even you!* Then Jimmy's face will fall because he will be forced to reflect on the fact that others can see and judge his face as he has judged Mrs. Smith's. And if he is like other children, he will run nervously to the nearest mirror in order to see exactly what other people see. Is his face acceptable? Is it safe? Does it adequately represent who he is? There begins the insecurity, the uncertainty, the self-consciousness, the lifelong war with the world at large. Childhood is the dawning of understanding that the world is set up in ways that would force one to bend or subjugate one's own will to the will of society. This is why I love children: I feel for them. And this is the main reason I don't have them. I, who found the will of society so oppressive in my own childhood, sympathize too much with their painful predicament.

I'm strong in many things, but when it comes to children and their struggles I have no strength. I cannot stand to see a child I love suffer. When I see my teenage nieces and nephews cry because of some insult or slight or rejection, I feel a terrible cold pain that turns hot and then cold again in the span of a few seconds. It's a sickening feeling of helplessness mixed with a feeling of responsibility that I know I could never live up to. I often ask my brothers and sisters how they let their children go off to school alone in the morning in a world full of bullies and pederasts, drunk drivers and drive-by shooters. I would not be able to let my child leave the house without a helmet on his head until he was thirty years old. I would have to follow him around everywhere he went, safeguarding him from everything that could cause him harm or suffering. I would be unhinged by the dangers he faced and would be so overprotective I fear I would destroy him and myself in the process. One day my sister's son (who understood he was gay but was still desperately trying to hide that fact from the world) came home from the fifth grade in tears because some boys from his class had followed him home and thrown stones at him and called him "faggot." My sister, a tall, powerful woman with a formidable sense of justice, asked her son which boy was the ringleader in this sordid attack. As soon as my nephew named the boy, she jumped into her car, drove to his house, and rang the doorbell.

When the boy opened the door, she said, "Hi, Bobby. Is your mother home?" Bobby said no, his mother was not home right now. Unable to address his mother in the civil manner she had intended, my sister took the next best option. She seized Bobby by his shirtfront and gave him a shaking impressive enough that a couple of buttons popped off the shirt, his teeth clacked, and the baseball cap flew off his head. When she was done with that, she held her index finger half an inch from his quivering lip and growled, "Don't you *ever* touch my son again!"

To my mind this punishment was much too light. Had it been my son who was harassed and taunted, I would have given Bobby a taste of his own medicine and *stoned* him to a slow, painful death. Though the thought alone is grossly inappropriate, twenty years later, I still occasionally have a desire to stone that boy.

Children learn quickly that they can expect unconditional love only from their parents. To reassure themselves that they are secure in that love, they test it, push it, measure it, and test themselves against it. The parent is the only person they can cross and vex with such volume and constancy without getting an injunction to go to hell and never come back. My brother, frustrated at his four-year-old son's behavior, said to me once through gritted teeth, "Sometimes you wish you could take a bullwhip and snap your child's cheek with it." He thought about this for a second as he watched his son ruin his expensive new school shoes by wading into Narragansett Bay with them, though the boy had been admonished six times not to do this. And then my brother said, "But of course, you can't whip your kids. You love them too much. You *have* to love them, no matter what asshole things they do. The whole thing is evolutionarily set up that way."

As I got deeper and deeper into the artificial insemination process, I was beginning to realize that it was precisely that unavoidable, slavish, evolutionary devotion that worried me. I knew I would not be strong enough to resist it. I would become, to my discredit, entirely servile. I would become my child's victim, and, as a result, he would become mine. Nathaniel Hawthorne's wife, Sophia, detailed the parental qualities necessary for good child rearing: "Infinite patience, infinite tenderness, infinite magnanimity—no less will do, and we must practise them as far as finite power will allow." She was right, of course, but what she was defining is no less than a superhuman state. I know there are people who can actually achieve that state. I also know that I cannot. I'm not half super enough. I'm too sensitive and nervous. Small things can upset me for days. I am a person who, by design, spends an inordinate amount of time alone, because too much constant contact with other people unsettles me. It's impossible for me to work if another person is in the house with me. I am distractible and easily thrown off key.

All this perhaps sounds precious, childish, and self-indulgent. But it's the opposite, believe me. It's a confession of a discouraging, adult piece of self-knowledge. I am self-doubting, and laden with guilt. I would never be able to say to my child, "Go away for two weeks while I sit at my desk."

(In fact, I would find it difficult to say to my child, "Go away for two hours.") To abandon a child in favor of one's personal desires or ambitions, as many male (and not a few female) parents have done, is, in my view, to commit the worst sort of crime. The one who brings a child into the world has a responsibility to give the child everything, to put the child before all else.

One day, soon after I turned forty-one, my doctor called me while I was driving to pick my niece up at school. I was pregnant. I stopped the car in the middle of the street to listen to her. She persuaded me that it was true, said, "Boy, did *you* beat all the odds," and suddenly I found myself incredibly confused. Pregnant? What did that mean? I felt as I imagine people feel when they win the lottery—thrilled by this huge thing but not quite able to take it in and not sure exactly how it will change their lives. After all that time and work trying to become pregnant, one would think I'd have been prepared. I wasn't. That first day I was delighted, beside myself with happiness, wandering around the house in a pleasing fog of anticipation. And yet the next day I woke up horrified. I got out of bed and stared out the window at the elementary school across the street from my house and thought, *This is a big mistake*. But then the next day I was thrilled again, barely able to keep myself from telling complete strangers about it. And the next day I was horrified.

It went on like that for weeks, my mood about the pregnancy swerving wildly from elation to horror. I went to the doctor for a checkup, and when she asked me if I wanted to hear the heartbeat, I was surprised to realize there was a heartbeat so early. I put on the stethoscope and listened, and my head actually reared back a little when I heard how loud and ambitious that half-Irish, half-Iranian heartbeat was. It was a crisp, rapid thumping, like a soldier's boots marching purposefully across a wooden bridge. It startled me for a second, and then I understood that the tiny fetus, no bigger than a walnut, was doing all it could to survive. Which made me adore it and thrilled me more than ever.

The very next day, though, I was decidedly unthrilled. I was worried, doubtful, anxious, and on the verge of tears all day. Now the child was real, and it was dawning on me that while worse people than I have been mothers, I was not suited to the task of raising a child, especially by myself. Days went by and I went on schizophrenically careering between happiness and dread. Finally, after thirteen weeks, I had a miscarriage. My disappointment was acute. All that miraculous genetic and biological complexity that would have flowered into a being with a distinct personality was brought to a premature end. It seemed to me no less tragic and colossal than a universe coming to an end. I was devastated by it for days. But when my doctor eventually asked me, with palpable zeal in her voice, if I wanted to try it again, I said no with complete conviction. I'd had to come nearly face-to-face with my own child to know that I did not want to be, nor believe I could be, anyone's mother.

I wish I had more equanimity, but I can't be someone I am

not. Life is such a complex, treacherous matter, so quickly lived and difficult to experience fully *precisely* because it is so crowded with diversity and choice. I decided to live what was left of my life in my own extreme, lopsided way and spare my child my worries and neuroses.

Parenting is, I think, the highest art. And the hardest. Few people master it. For me, it was a moment of clarity and foresight when I realized that those footsteps I heard marching boldly across the bridge in my doctor's office that day would one day be marching beside me, and that my overpowering desire would be to carry the child in my arms forever so he wouldn't have to walk. I can't know how it might have turned out if I had persisted and finally had a child, but I am fifty-three years old now and I do know this: when I find myself walking up a mountain path alone, I have no regret.

JUST AN AUNT

by

Elliott Holt

WHAT DO YOU WEAR to a state psychiatric hospital? *Nothing too revealing*, says the visitor's guide. *Nothing gang-related or obscene.* I am wearing black corduroys and a boyish gray sweater. Black Converse sneakers, no earrings, no lipstick. I've pulled my hair into one long braid. It's a winter evening, not even six, but the sun is long gone. At the security gate, the guard who asks for my ID has a Russian accent. *"Gavorite po-russki?"* I ask as I hand him my driver's license. Do you speak Russian? His eyes light up. *"Da,"* he says. In his mother tongue, he directs me to the hospital: right, then down Dogwood Drive—a pleasant name for such a dark, desolate stretch of pavement—through another security gate toward the new building with the copper facade. At the front desk, a chipper woman greets me. I'm here to help with a women's writing group. "I'm sorry I'm late," I say. "I got a little lost." "You don't want to be lost on Alabama Avenue," says one of the armed guards with a knowing laugh. "No," I say conspiratorially. "I guess not." St. Elizabeths is on Alabama Avenue SE, on the other side of the Anacostia River from the Washington I know. I grew up in Northwest D.C., the leafy, sheltered quadrant of the city that is mostly white, mostly rich. This part of Southeast might as well be another city. The guards usher me through the metal detector and open my bag. It is not like being in an airport, though. The security guards are joking and warm: quick to establish a rapport with me. Perhaps they sense that I am nervous, or perhaps they just want to remind me that we are on the same sane team. *We're not like the ones inside*, they seem to say.

Many of the ones inside this hospital are NGBRI (not guilty by reason of insanity). They have personality disorders and a history of psychotic breaks. They're here because they are a danger to others, and to themselves. I'm not like the ones inside, but my own complicated psychiatric history is what brought me here, as a curious and empathetic volunteer. I have never been psychotic. I have never suffered from delusions or other breaks from reality. But I have long been crippled by dark moods, paralyzed by existential dread. I've suffered several major depressive episodes in my life, the most recent of which lasted nearly two years and was especially terrifying.

The fact that I don't have kids is less the result of a decision than a collapse. I fell into a deep, dark depression at the age of thirty-six, when my fertility was already on the wane, and when, if I'd really wanted children, I would have had to make parenthood—with a partner or alone—a priority. I'm now very relieved that I don't have children. I recently tried running with a jogging stroller, while babysitting my infant nephew, and found the process so awkward and slow that I vowed never to do it again. I don't want my running stride—or anything else—hampered by children. When people ask why I don't have kids, I sometimes say, "I'm forty; that ship has sailed." Or I say, "I'm focused on producing books, not children." Or, "I can't afford to have a child on my own." That's all true; it's just not the full story.

In my early thirties, I thought I wanted kids. Most of my friends were having children. (I hosted five different baby showers between 2006 and 2010, and attended at least twenty-five more. I've spent thousands of dollars on tiny outfits and charming bath toys.) Watching my friends marry and reproduce while I remained single and childless made me feel like a foreign exchange student: I could understand some of the language of coupledom and parenthood, but I was not a native speaker, and I was always trying to catch up in conversations. "Having kids gives you perspective," a friend once said to me, smugly, in response to my worries about what he considered a minor problem. He wasn't the first person to make me feel like my childless state was a character flaw. I felt pressure to have kids from every side. It didn't help that I lived in Park Slope, Brooklyn, a neighborhood defined by parenthood.

I figured I'd be a good mother. As the oldest child in my family, I'd always looked after my siblings. I taught my youngest sister to read, to ride a bike. I was in the hospital room when my oldest niece was born seven years ago, and watching her swim into the world activated all my maternal instincts. I was thirty-three, and a month later, I broke up with my boyfriend at the time because he didn't want kids.

I'm a devoted aunt. I now have three nieces and one nephew. I've changed diapers; I've read bedtime stories. I've gone to school assemblies and stayed up late wrapping Christmas presents from Santa. I've helped my nieces sound out new words in books and reminded them to chew with their mouths closed. The girls rely on me, for comfort and answers, as if I were a third parent. But when I'm in the throes of writing I don't have to stop working to take care of the kids. I don't have to apologize for staying at my desk for twelve hours straight. (I feel most like myself when I have a pen in my hand.) When I'm worried about money—like most writers I know, I'm always worried about money, and always trying to find more freelance work—I know that my financial instability isn't going to hurt a child. I'm not responsible for school tuition or pediatrician bills. I can take off for a month at a time, to an artists' residency or colony, without any guilt. It's freeing to be an artist who only has to take care of making art. But most important, if I have another debilitating depression, I won't endanger any kids. I've survived all my depressive episodes. But what if, someday, I reach a point at which the psychic pain is too much to bear?

"What's my diagnosis?" I asked my shrink last year. It's a question I'd been afraid to ask for years. I've seen many psychologists and psychiatrists. All doctors put a code, representing a diagnosis, on the insurance bill. But I've never wanted to know what those codes mean. When I was an adolescent, one doctor deemed me "anxious/depressed." I imagined myself hovering in that slash, a fluid boundary between worry and melancholy. But in the intervening years, I've been reluctant to find out if that diagnosis is still true. I know I'm anxious and inclined to get depressed, but I'm always afraid that something worse is lurking in the recesses of my brain. What if, God forbid, I have a personality disorder and don't know about it? "Depressed mood, with adjustment disorder" is what the doctor told me. Which basically means that I'm not good at transitions. It makes sense, the doctor said, given the lack of stability in my childhood home. I need consistency in my life. As far as mood disorders go, mine is mild. "Do you think of yourself as mentally ill?" my doctor once asked me. "Don't *you* consider me mentally ill?" I said. "No," he said. (That was news to me, but I've always been my own worst critic.) But I lack the resilience necessary to cope with change. Moves, breakups, and other life changes can lead to depression.

It was a breakup that precipitated the deepest depression I've ever experienced. I can't explain why the end of that particular relationship caused me so much pain. It was partly because I had allowed myself to believe in a future with that man. He often began sentences with "When we get married . . ." He said, "Having a child with you would be a wonderful adventure." But the breakup was also devastating because I'd lost so much of myself with him. The romance fed my ego—no one had pursued me more aggressively, or made me feel so desired—and when it ended, as suddenly as it had begun fourteen months earlier, I felt crushed and disposable. I also felt humiliated. Our relationship unraveled partly because I dreamed of marriage and children and he, who already had a child and was going through a divorce, understandably cooled on the idea of both. It wasn't his fault that I had unrealistic expectations. I was nearly thirty-seven, and knew that if I wanted to be a mother, I didn't have time to waste. But when he broke up with me, I fell into such an abyss that I wasn't sure I'd ever pull myself out.

I understand now that what I suffered then can only be described as a nervous breakdown. I was nervous—so nervous I couldn't eat, and lost nearly twenty pounds—and I was broken. Not just my heart, though that was the location of the original crack. My brain felt broken, too. I couldn't think clearly; I couldn't sleep. I was sure I deserved this punishment. *Of course he left me,* I thought. *Why would he want to be with me, when he could find a more stable, perky partner?* At night, I often took the Klonopin my doctor had prescribed for insomnia and hoped that I'd never wake up. I was so depressed that I couldn't get out of bed to brush my teeth at night. *Let them rot,* I thought. I no longer cared. I dreamed regularly of my teeth crumbling and falling out, a symptom of my body's decay.

In those days, I took a lot of scalding baths. I'd grab a book—books have always been my most reliable companions—and sink into my claw-foot tub. I read until the water turned tepid, then dropped the book on the floor and catalogued my sins. I leaned my head back and let my hair spread like seaweed. Underwater, I imagined that I was swimming—I am a strong swimmer, even in oceans—but there were moments when I realized how easily I could drown. I could just let go. Let my body fill with water, let it green with bloat.

Virginia Woolf's suicide note read in part: "I feel certain that I am going mad again. I feel we can't go through another one of those terrible times. And I shan't recover this time. I begin to hear voices, and I can't concentrate. So I am doing what seems the best thing to do." Every time I read that note, I'm glad that Woolf didn't have children. (She was, like me, a doting aunt.) But I'm also relieved that I've never heard voices. I like to think that I have never crossed from pain to madness, though there have been times when I felt like I was losing my mind—losing its clarity and focus. And in my darkest depression, there were days—months, actually—when life seemed so dire that I understood exactly what Woolf meant when she wrote, "I can't fight anymore."

I didn't give up on life because I couldn't bear to hurt my family. And because I adopted a dog who got me out of bed in the morning. I had to walk him; I had to feed him. He loved me unconditionally, and taking care of him saved me. As I clawed my way out of the dark hole (with help from my sisters, a therapist, antidepressants, and long walks in the woods with my dog), I vowed never again to let my happiness depend on a romantic relationship. I realized that I cared more about writing a book than about having a baby. I stopped thinking about love and instead focused my energy on finishing my novel. I haven't been in a relationship since that one ended, but I did publish a book.

My first visit to a mental hospital, in 1988, was not voluntary. I was in eighth grade and my parents thought I was suicidal. The memories of the night on which they committed me are vague: I've blocked a lot of it out. I know that I arrived at the hospital wearing a pair of new Guess? jeans. Jeans I'd begged my mother to buy, despite the fact that my parents didn't have money to spend on designer clothes. I was desperate to belong, and belonging in those days meant wearing Guess? and Benetton. I was unusually skinny for my age: I weighed, at fourteen, just under eighty pounds. And the jeans, which were size 0, were held up with a belt. The belt, along with my shoelaces, and my jar of Noxema, was confiscated from me when I arrived at the hospital. Apparently, even a tub of skin cream can be a weapon of self-destruction in determined hands. Being on suicide watch means constant surveillance. Doors have to remain open; you can't even go to the bathroom without supervision. And so I spent my first night, imprisoned, and awoke in the morning to find myself among patients who struck me as insane.

I was in the ICU, on a ward with five other teenagers and about ten adults. One boy, just a few years older than I, seemed manic. He showed me the scars on his wrists from a suicide attempt. A middle-aged woman saw the triangle logo on my butt and said, "Those Guess? jeans?" I must have said yes. (And I must have been holding the jeans up, since I no longer had a belt.) "You must be rich," she said. I didn't bother to explain that at my school, I wasn't rich enough. The kids who were cruel to me (I still remember girls at a fifth-grade slumber party repeating, "You suck, Elliott," as I cried inside my sleeping bag) were rich. My classmates boasted of vacations to Jamaica and Aspen. Their parents picked them up in Mercedes and Maseratis. My parents fretted about whether they'd be able to pay our school tuition. Since I was nine, my underemployed father had been saying things like, "I should just kill myself. You'd all be better off with the insurance money." I was too young to know that he didn't really mean it. My father is a brilliant, kind man and I never doubted that he would do anything for us. But he was lonely and overwhelmed, taking care of three girls on his own; my mother was rarely home.

My mother was nurturing and fun, but she was also in East Africa for four months of every year. She was a financial analyst at the World Bank, focused on infrastructure projects that took her on month-long "missions," as the bank called them, during which she was completely out of touch.

There was no Internet; there were no satellite phones. My two younger sisters and I were, in effect, without a mother a third of the year. While she was gone, my father retired to his bedroom early in the evening. "I'm going to lie down for a while," he'd say. My sisters and I would find him fully dressed in the fetal position, asleep on top of the comforter. In the middle of the night, while we were asleep, he'd wake up and go to the grocery store. It's painful to imagine him in the empty fluorescent aisles of the Georgetown Safeway at three o'clock in the morning, hunting and gathering in his own stunted way.

In committing me to the hospital, my parents called my bluff. I'd threatened to kill myself. When they told me they would take me to the hospital, I threatened to kill myself right there, in the kitchen, with a knife I grabbed from the counter. The knife was a prop, but I used it convincingly. I had dramatic tendencies. Like a lot of adolescents, I didn't actually want to die. I wanted to be missed. My ideations were not about suicide, per se, but about the funeral that might be held for me. I liked to imagine my classmates, chastened; I liked to think that everyone who had been mean to me would be sorry if I were dead. That blurry night was the culmination of a terrible year. A year in which I was often in tears, and often in a rage fueled by grief. I missed my mother. I was socially ostracized; school had become so painful that I'd stopped doing my homework. I, who had always been a perfect student, was now so unprepared for my final exams that I was certain I'd fail. It was the end of the school year, my last year at the school I'd attended since I was four. I was anxious about changing schools. And I was desperate for help. "You're sick," my mother said. At some point that night, I stopped fighting. I sank down on the kitchen floor, let the dog lick my teary face. I don't know which parent put the knife away. I know that I finally agreed to go upstairs and pack a bag.

In the psychiatric hospital, it was a relief to see the other patients as crazy. I must be sane, I thought, because I couldn't recognize the behavior around me. In my first group therapy session with the other teens, I said nothing. I didn't want to share my feelings with a roomful of strangers. The doctor told me I'd never get out if I didn't speak "in group." When my parents came to visit later that day, I demanded my release because I knew I didn't belong there. My parents must have known the same thing, because just two days after they checked me in to the hospital, they checked me out. That was my first and last stay in a psych ward.

My mother warned me never to tell anyone I'd been in the asylum. She was afraid of the stigma. My mother valued reason above all. She sometimes said of her own mother, "She's too emotional" or "She's not rational." I worshipped my mother, and knew that my intense emotional responses to the world were a disappointment to her. I don't blame her for sending me to the hospital. She was scared; if my child were that depressed, I might react the same way. But when she committed me to the psych ward, I felt exiled. And when she warned me to keep the episode secret, I felt deeply ashamed. I've felt, ever since, like something is wrong with me. My view of myself as fucked up comes less from the actual hospitalization than from my mother's reaction to it.

I had other depressive episodes. In tenth grade, I couldn't write my English term paper. I had stacks of index cards filled with my notes and quotes from Thomas Hardy's *Tess of the d'Urbervilles*, but I couldn't focus enough to write the essay. It was my first long paper and I wanted it to be perfect. As the deadline approached, I panicked. I couldn't sleep. I stayed up all night watching black-and-white reruns on Nick at Nite. I watched *Leave It to Beaver* and *The Donna Reed Show* and other innocent programs from my parents' childhood. At dawn, when my younger sisters got up for school, I was still on the couch downstairs in our sunroom. As they sat down to breakfast, I turned off the TV and went up to bed. The term paper's due date came and went. My parents told the school I was sick, and I was. But it was not a physical ailment; it was my mind that was in torment. For weeks, I stayed up all night and then slept all day. I never wrote that paper, so I got a D in English that semester. I was certain that I had destroyed my future. And during one rocky semester in college, on an art history exam for which I was not prepared, I filled the blue book with the lyrics from "Rocky Raccoon" by the Beatles, which strikes me now as lunatic behavior. I thought it was funny at the time.

But then I spent all of my twenties and most of my thirties in remission. I worked, successfully, at ad agencies in

Moscow, London, and New York. I got my MFA in fiction writing at night, at Brooklyn College, while working full-time at a Manhattan agency during the day. I met all my deadlines, got promotions, and won awards. I had melancholic periods, but I never collapsed under the self-doubt that paralyzed me as an adolescent. Even when my mother died of cancer, when I was thirty-one, I did not succumb to depression. I was grieving, but I was functioning. (This is largely due to the antidepressants I starting taking right after she died. Going on antidepressants was, for me, a revelation. If only I'd been medicated sooner, I'm sure my GPA would have been higher. I function so much better on Zoloft that I will never go off medication again.) The reality is that depressed people often function well in their twenties and thirties. As they age, however, depression becomes harder to treat. As Peter D. Kramer put it in *Against Depression*, "bouts of depression recur with greater frequency. Later episodes can appear spontaneously, without apparent reason. They last longer, respond poorly to any intervention, remit (when they do) more briefly." Now that I'm forty, my depression has the potential to be increasingly dangerous to my health. And as a woman with a history of anxiety and depression, I'd be at risk for postpartum depression. Suicide is the leading cause of death in new mothers. I'd rather not take that chance.

Recently, when I was giving my four-year-old niece a bath, she said, "I'm not sure I want to have kids. I just want to be an aunt." What sparked this remark, I don't know. Does she sense how much sacrifice is involved in raising children? Like me at her age, my niece spends most of her time making up stories and songs. She has an unusual dexterity with language. She is a natural storyteller, with an innate sense of pacing. She is already constructing artful sentences. I wonder if she, too, will devote herself to writing. "You don't have to decide that now," I said. "Someday you can have kids if you want."

What kind of mother would I have been? A worried one, no doubt. My sisters and I often joke about how high-strung I am. When I was in my early twenties, my youngest sister said to me, "You can only have kids if you go running every day." For me, exercise has always been essential to managing my moods. (I stopped running regularly during that last ill-fated relationship and I'm quite sure that if I had started again after our breakup, I would have been far less depressed.) I thrive on routine, so I would have insisted on a structured existence for my children: precise bedtimes and lots of scheduled activities. I'm sure I would have fretted about developmental milestones ("Shouldn't she be reading already?") and, like my own overachieving parents, taken too much pride in my children's accomplishments. I'm a perfectionist, so I fear that I would have expected too much of my kids. But I would have read to them every day, even when they were infants. And I would have sung the lullabies my mother always sang to me: "Dona Dona Dona" and "Me and Bobby McGee."

My sisters are good mothers. The one with three girls is a stay-at-home mom. Her days are, like so many parents', parceled into drop-offs and pickups, from school, from birthday parties, from swim practices and soccer games. She is the reluctant pilot of a minivan. My sister's devotion to her kids is partly a reaction to our childhood; she is trying to give her own children the emotional stability we lacked. I offer my three nieces an entirely different female model: a career-focused artist, with no financial security, who will probably never own a house. My nieces have seen my novel in bookstores. The oldest proudly told her first-grade class that her "aunt is an author." I want the girls to understand that it is possible to be both a professional woman and a parent, but I can't be the one to set that example. As the four-year-old already understands, not all girls grow up to be mothers.

If I hadn't felt abandoned by my own mother, if I'd been more lucky in love, if I'd published my first book when I was younger, if I were, by nature, less sensitive and more confident, perhaps I would have tried to have children. But I can't complain: I'm alive and thriving. And even without kids, I have plenty of perspective.

At St. Elizabeths, one of the women in the writing group took my hand. "What are you afraid of, the dark?" she asked. It was her first question. She didn't ask me where I went to school or what I do for a living. She didn't care if I was married or had children. In the psych hospital, we immediately got down to the raw, unfiltered business of being human. On some level, aren't we all afraid of the dark?

THE END OF THE LINE

by

Tim Kreider

I RECENTLY SAW a *New Yorker* cover drawn by my old colleague Ivan Brunetti that appeared to illustrate the nonexistent situation of a couple of hipsters in a chic eatery looking wistfully at a middle-aged couple schlepping home with their children in Halloween costumes, carrying a boxed pizza for dinner. At first I assumed this was a kind of naive wishfulfillment on the part of parents, incorrectly imagining that anybody envies them. It took me a day or two to understand that although the cover was drawn from the visual point of view of the hipsters, it was drawn from the *emotional* point of view of the parents, who are relieved to be looking comfortably schlubby and going home for a night of candy and takeout with their kids instead of having to get all dolled up and go on a date at some fashionable tapas bar for an over-priced gourmet morsel. This I can understand.

Parents may frequently look back with envy on the ir-responsible, self-indulgent lives of the childless, but I for one have never felt any reciprocal envy of their anxious and harried existence—noisy and toy-strewn, pee-stained and shrieky, without two consecutive moments to read a book or have an adult conversation or formulate a coherent thought. In an essay, I once described being a parent as like belong-ing to a cult, "living in conditions of appalling filth and deg-radation, subject to the whim of a capricious and demented master," which a surprising number of parents told me they loved. It's hard to imagine the electively childless respond-ing as warmly to an equally unsympathetic description of their own lives. This is because parents still remember what it was like to be us, but we can't imagine what it's like to be them; their experience encompasses ours. I accept that people with children are having a deeper, more complex experi-ence of being alive than I am, and this is fine with me. Raising children is one of many life experiences I'm happy to die with-out having had, like giving birth, going to war, spending a night in jail, or seeing *Forrest Gump*. If I could get through life without experiencing death, I would gladly do that, too.

All living things on this planet have a simple two-part mission: to (1) survive long enough to (2) self-replicate. It is a complex animal indeed, arguably one too highly evolved for its own good, that consciously declines to fulfill one of its few basic biological imperatives. The only act more perverse and unnatural than purposely not reproducing is suicide. Some philosophers—the really crabby ones, like Schopenhauer—define suicide as the ultimate act of moral choice and free will. And, some ambiguous anecdotes aside, it appears to be the exclusive prerogative of *Homo sapiens*. I suppose you could argue that choosing not to have children, like suicide, is uniquely human. In fact, if anything can be said to demonstrate the possibility of free will, it is this: human beings willfully thwarting their one predetermined function in life.

Admittedly, calling not having children the ultimate act of free will may be a little grandiose. People on both sides of the reproductive divide tend to be self-congratulatory about choices that are, let's be honest, completely beyond their conscious control, like people who've inherited wealth thinking they deserve it. Parents need to somehow justify the lives of sputum, tuition, and sarcastic abuse to which they've condemned themselves, and so make their own grandiose claims about parenthood's ineffable fulfillments and beneficent effects—that one cannot possibly know what real love is unless you've had children, that it is life's ultimate purpose, et cetera.

Reproduction as raison d'être has always seemed to me to beg the whole question of existence. If the ultimate purpose of your life is your children, what's the purpose of your children's lives? To have your grandchildren? Isn't anyone's life ultimately meaningful in itself? If not, what's the point of propagating it ad infinitum? After all, $0 \times \infty = 0$. It would seem a pretty low-rent ultimate purpose that's shared with viruses and bacteria. The current human population is descended from a relatively low number of ancestors after a series of population bottlenecks in the late Pleistocene. Most human beings back then presumably felt their lives to be just as important and meaningful as we do ours. Is their existence negated just because they left no descendants?

In any case, children are no guarantee of immortality—they're only a genetic reprieve or extension at best. Eventually the species *Homo sapiens* will die off, and even if we escape the sun's expansion into a red giant and colonize another star system or download our consciousness into machines or evolve into pure energy life forms, eventually (according to current consensus) the universe itself will undramatically gutter out in a boring heat death and everyone—your kids, their kids, your great(23)-grandchildren, Shakespeare, Beethoven, Lincoln, Nietzsche, Akira Kurosawa, and me—will be even more utterly nonexistent than completely forgotten, since there won't even be anyone around to forget us.

The childless, on the other hand—or *childfree*, as the more aggressive ones like to be called (a formation apparently derived from the uncomplimentary *smoke-* and *disease-free*)—like to claim that they're living more fully conscious lives than those brainless docile hordes helplessly breeding at the dictates of their DNA. They cite the imminent threats of overpopulation, global warming, peak oil, and, don't let's forget, nuclear war, still very much on the table—all of which are perfectly valid and persuasive reasons for not procreating, and none of which do I believe for one second is anyone's real reason. Our real reasons may be less obvious than those of parents—or the *child-curs'd*, as we like to call them—but I have no doubt they're just as unconscious and primal. The rise in voluntary childlessness, like the decrease in fertility and the increase in homosexuality, may be an evolutionary adaptation to overpopulation.* Or, since the phenomenon is more prevalent in the West, maybe it's an effect of wealth and plenty. (Having more offspring is to an individual's evolutionary advantage in impoverished conditions, even though it's disastrous for the species as a whole and has made places like Rio and Calcutta some of the least desirable real estate in the solar system.) Or perhaps it's a symptom of a civilization in its decadence, a loss of vitality or optimism. Or maybe bad parenting, like vampirism, grows exponentially with each new generation, and we've finally reached a critical mass of people whose own childhoods were so lousy they've taken Philip Larkin's famously dour advice: "Don't have any kids yourself."

All the best arguments that parents and the childless muster about which of their lives is the more rational, satisfying, and/or morally superior are about as interesting to me as the ongoing debate about Which Are Better: Cats or Dogs. Our most important decisions in life are all profoundly irrational ones, made subconsciously for reasons we seldom own up to,

---

*The fertility rate has been declining, even in the third world, since the 1950s. Whether the incidence of homosexuality has been increasing in humans is impossible to gauge, but rats in deliberately overpopulated lab conditions exhibit increased homosexual behavior in subsequent generations.

which is why the worst ideas (getting married for the third time, having an affair with your wife's sister, secretly going off birth control as your marriage is collapsing) are the most impossible to talk anyone out of. It's pointless to refute all the rhapsodic slop about how kids make your life meaningful, since it's all pretty obviously rationalization, like the perfectly sensible reasons people offer for carrying out post-hypnotic suggestions. There is one reason people have children: they're programmed to. Whatever reasons they may offer for it—selflessness, wanting to pass something on, having so much love to give—I don't believe they choose children any more than naked mole rats decide to start tunneling. Human beings are basically big complicated Rube Goldberg contraptions constructed by genes to copy themselves, and only as an unintended side effect build mosques, make screwball comedies, and launch interplanetary probes.

I know, for my own part, that not having children wasn't the consequence of some carefully deliberated decision, taking into account the world population, my bleak economic future, or my incapacity to take care of anything more demanding than a cat. It simply never even once occurred to me to have children, any more than it ever occurred to me to enlist in the Coast Guard or take up Brazilian jujitsu. I never understood why anyone else *was* doing it; I did not get what was even supposed to be fun or fulfilling or whatever it was about parenting that compelled everyone else to do it. Everyone seemed to have agreed, on some day of class I missed, that this was obviously the thing to do. Who knows why I'm devoid of such a nearly universal human impulse? I always intended to be an artist, and never imagined a wife or children in any future I envisioned—though this is such a pragmatic rationale it's obviously suspect, and, after all, plenty of other artists have had families and been just as indifferent and distracted as parents with day jobs. My own upbringing was fine, although I was given up for adoption when I was a few days old, which, I've since read, can do something of a number on a kid. My mother tells me I never liked babies, even when I was one. To this day, whenever someone asks me whether I'd like to hold the baby, I always answer, "No, thanks." I have been advised that this is an impolitic response. Not long ago my friend Zoey made me hold her one-year-old and took photos of me. Wincing gamely with the kicking child on my lap, I felt the way I imagine women do when their boyfriends cajole them into dressing up as Catholic schoolgirls or Princess Leia, indulging some fantasy that has nothing to do with them. Later she sent me the photos as "proof" that I am not such a bad man after all. To me, I look in these photos as if I am holding some South American animal I have never heard of before that I've been assured is not dangerous.

Suffice it to say this has sometimes been an Issue in relationships with women, most of whom sooner or later seem to want kids. Somewhere in my thirties I started preemptively letting women know that I had no interest in having children, had never considered it, not for one second, and there was absolutely no chance I was ever going to change

my mind, not even if the Right Person were to come along.
It must've seemed as if I was being gratuitously blunt about
this, but in my experience people have a bottomless capacity
to delude themselves that their partners will eventually
change. This policy didn't exactly end any relationships, but
it did obviate some potential ones, and/or kept others circumscribed. But whatever awkwardness it's occasioned me is
nothing compared to the suffocating societal pressure that
women who don't want children are subjected to. After all,
there's a sort of role model or template for a man who doesn't
want kids—the Confirmed Bachelor, roguish and irascible
in the W. C. Fields tradition. At worst, we're considered
selfish or immature; women who don't want to have children
are regarded as unnatural, traitors to their sex, if not the
species. Men who don't want kids get a dismissive eye roll,
but the reaction to women who don't want them is more
like: *What's wrong with you?*

Having children is self-evidently the less rational decision—hugely expensive and inconvenient, consistently dem-
onstrated in studies to increase stress and reduce happiness
both in individuals and between couples. A friend who's currently writing a novel about the widening divide between
people who have children and their friends who don't, and
who is himself childless, asked his friends with kids to help
him out and explain to him the appeal of having children.
The cons were evident; what, he wondered, were the pros?
They admitted that yes, it was exhausting, they drove you
crazy, you never had a free moment, but, they'd say, "When

your child smiles at you, it just makes it all worth it somehow." He had no fucking idea what they were talking about.
To be fair, he said, they all seemed aware that they were grop-
ing for the goopiest clichés to describe the experience: "They
were like someone trying to explain an acid trip in which It
All Made Sense, even as they realized that you had to be
there." It's apparently something either so ineffable or primal that it resists articulation.

Of course most people are inarticulate on all subjects, especially the profoundest ones; it may be instructive to listen
to what some of our most hyperarticulate artists have had to
say about parenthood. Even that old sourpuss Cormac Mc-
Carthy seems to have been transformed by fatherhood; his
novel *The Road*, best known for its unrelieved bleakness (it
includes flayed babies roasted on spits), is the first in which
he's written convincingly about a truly loving relationship (as
opposed to an obsessive *Liebestod* for a beautiful doomed pros-
titute or the enduring bond between a boy and his wolf): the
love the nameless protagonist feels for his fragile, ineduca-
bly decent son, a love that redeems the world even in the face
of extinction. *If he is not the word of God, God never spoke.* The
book's fundamental question is, what, if anything, makes
life worth slogging on with, given the fact of inevitable and
universal death? His only answer is: this child does.

Most people's operating motive in life is pretty obviously
not the pleasure principle, given the joyless choices they make;
what they want is to be needed, to have a compelling reason to get out of bed every day. If having children doesn't

necessarily provide meaning, it's certainly an effective way to obviate, or at least postpone, the question of meaning throughout the prime years of life. You may wake up at four A.M. panicked about the mortgage payments or want to hang yourself rather than go in to work one more day, but too bad, it doesn't matter; you have to keep putting one foot in front of the other, because your child is depending upon you. Whereas there's really nothing stopping me, on any given Tuesday morning, from taking up heroin. All this maundering about What Is Life for, Anyway is a luxury of the unencumbered. Children serve as an inarguable rebuttal to all those existential anxieties and doubts. As one noted American philosopher put it: "You're nobody 'til somebody loves you."

It wasn't until relatively late in life, when I met people I was biologically related to for the first time, that I had some glimmering of how parents must feel about their children. I like my half sisters enormously as human beings; they're smart, funny, kindhearted girls, and we're similar in ways that feel deeply familiar to me (I'd never noticed the obvious etymology of *familiar* before). But I also adore them in a gushy, ferocious, unconditional way that has nothing to do with who they are but with what they are to me. I would love them just as much if they were junkies or Republicans or thought I was creepy and wanted nothing to do with me. When I look over at one of them next to me in a car or at a party I secretly thrill with a warm, narcotic love. If one of them needed a kidney, I would give her one; if the other one needed one, I would, with some regret, give her the other. It makes me so happy just to know that they exist that I can almost empathize with the weirdly ecstatic reactions of grandparents to the unremarkable toddlers produced by their own children. It gives me a glimpse of what having children might be like, and also of what I would be like as a father—doting and indulgent, pathetically mushy with love. And I have to admit to myself that although I have plenty of sound reasons for not being a father—I know I would also be inconsistent and moody, alternately smothering and neglectful, plus I will never, ever be able to afford riding lessons or braces, let alone college—one of the reasons I don't want children is fear. I'm afraid that if I ever did have children of my own I would love them so painfully it would rip my soul in half, that I would never again have a waking moment free from the terror that something bad might ever happen to them. Some friends of mine lost their young daughter a few years ago; most people, me included, recoil from even trying to imagine what they've suffered.

Is it possible that I will regret not having had children when I am old and dying alone? People with children love to ask this of us childless types, the way evangelicals like to imagine your tearful deathbed repentance or belated contrition in Hell. Since I already regret every other thing I have ever done or failed to do, I don't see why this decision should be exempt. Sure: no doubt I will realize, once it's far too late, as usual, that I have failed to do the one dumb job it was my charge to do during my brief time on the planet, a job countless fungi, flatworms, and imbeciles have successfully carried out for eons. Perhaps at the eleventh hour I will convince a kindly nymphomaniac nurse, such as I understand to be a fixture at most hospitals, to bear whatever child my tattered chromosomes can produce. But I am long practiced at pursuing paths I know lead inevitably to regret. I am much too old and weird and selfish by now to endure the fatigue and anxiety of new parenthood, to feign enthusiasm for recitals and pageants and soccer matches, to be dragged uncomplainingly to Pixar sequels and Chuck E. Cheese's and American Girl stores.

Being childless is inarguably saner and more responsible in the present world situation than having children, but let's not pretend we're actually doing it for sane or responsible reasons. If the childless really feel a need to claim some moral superiority over the child-ridden, it should be simply by virtue of not kidding ourselves. Let's be honest: we *are* unnatural—as unnatural as clothing or medicine or agriculture or art, or walking upright. By not having progeny we are depriving ourselves of the illusion of continuity, and have to invest ourselves more deeply in other, more austere illusions: that our lives matter for their own sakes, or that we'll secure a kind of immortality through art or ideas or acts of decency, by teaching or helping others or changing the world. Maybe we're an evolutionary adaptation; spreading memes instead of genes is a more efficient means of reproduction, less destructive to the environment. We're propagating ourselves throughout the noosphere instead of lousing up an already overpopulated planet with yet more human beings.

The last century was the first time in history that a sizable percentage of the human race attempted to live without delusions of eternity; it was also the first time that any significant number of us voluntarily renounced procreation, abandoning the false consolation of posterity. (I wonder, sometimes, whether the negative population growth in the secular West might subconsciously be linked to the death of faith.) It's only very recently, within the last fifty years, that not having children has become a practical option, both medically and socially. Formerly, childlessness was seen as a private tragedy; the only people who chose it voluntarily were clergy, who, in theory, had religion to sublimate their erotic drive. We childless ones are an experiment unprecedented in human history. We are unlikely, for obvious reasons, to take over. Like the Shakers, who also declined on principle to procreate, individually we are doomed to extinction. Although so is everyone else. But as an option, an idea, who knows? We may thrive and spread. We are an object lesson—an existence theorem, which demonstrates that a proposition is possible—to the rest of the species. At the risk of sounding grandiose and self-congratulatory again, I'll venture to suggest that we childless ones, whether through bravery or cowardice, constitute a kind of existential vanguard, forced by our own choices to face the naked question of existence with fewer illusions, or at least fewer consolations, than the rest of humanity, forced to prove to ourselves anew every day that extinction does not negate meaning.

ACKNOWLEDGMENTS

For their guidance, wisdom, and careful greasing of various wheels, the editor would like to thank Anna deVries, P. J. Horoszko, Stephen Morrison, and Andrea Rogoff at Picador. Particular gratitude is owed to Hanya Yanagihara for putting this train on the tracks and monitoring its journey to a safe, though never too distant, future.

CONTRIBUTORS

MEGHAN DAUM, editor, is the author of four books, most recently *The Unspeakable: And Other Subjects of Discussion*, published in 2014 by Farrar, Straus and Giroux. Her other books are the essay collection *My Misspent Youth*, the novel *The Quality of Life Report*, and the memoir *Life Would Be Perfect If I Lived in That House*. An opinion columnist for the *Los Angeles Times* for nearly a decade, Meghan has written for *The New Yorker*, *Harper's*, *Elle*, and *Vogue*, among other publications. She lives in Los Angeles.

KATE CHRISTENSEN is the author, most recently, of *Blue Plate Special: An Autobiography of My Appetites*, as well as six novels, including *The Epicure's Lament* and *The Great Man*, which won the 2008 PEN/Faulkner Award for Fiction. She has published essays and reviews in numerous publications, among them *The New York Times Sunday Book Review*; *Elle*; *O, the Oprah Magazine*; *Martha Stewart Living*; and *Bookforum*. Her next book, *How to Cook a Moose*, will be published by Islandport Press in September 2015. She blogs about food and life in New England at katechristensen.wordpress.com. She lives in Portland, Maine.

GEOFF DYER's many books include *But Beautiful*, *Zona*, *Otherwise Known as the Human Condition*, and *Jeff in Venice, Death in Varanasi*. His books have been translated into twenty-four languages. He is currently living in Venice, California.

DANIELLE HENDERSON is a freelance writer who works with *The Guardian*, *Vulture*, *Rookie*, *Cosmopolitan*, and others. She created the *Feminist Ryan Gosling* blog and book before she left academia forever, and she hopes she is always the first person her best friends' children call for bail money and prophylactics. Born and raised in New York, Danielle now lives in Seattle.

COURTNEY HODELL is a book editor and the director of the Whiting Writers' Awards. She has worked at Viking, Random House, HarperCollins UK and US, and, most recently, as executive editor at Farrar, Straus and Giroux. She is the aunt of Elsa Symons-Hodell.

ANNA HOLMES is a writer and the author of two books, *Hell Hath No Fury: Women's Letters from the End of the Affair* and *The Book of Jezebel*, which was based on the popular website she created in 2007. She works as an editor for *Fusion* and as a contributing columnist for *The New York Times Sunday Book Review*.

ELLIOTT HOLT's short fiction and essays have appeared in *The New York Times*, *Virginia Quarterly Review*, *Guernica*, *Kenyon Review* online, and the 2011 Pushcart Prize anthology. Her first novel, *You Are One of Them* (Penguin Press, 2013), was a *New York Times Sunday Book Review* Editors' Choice and a finalist for the National Book Critics Circle's inaugural John Leonard Award.

PAM HOUSTON is the author of two novels, *Contents May Have Shifted* and *Sight Hound*; two collections of short stories, *Cowboys Are My Weakness* and *Waltzing the Cat*; and a collection of essays, *A Little More About Me*, all published by W. W. Norton. Her stories have been selected for volumes of the O. Henry Awards, the 2013 Pushcart Prize, and Best American Short Stories of the Century. She is a professor of English at UC Davis and directs the literary nonprofit Writing By Writers.

MICHELLE HUNEVEN is the author of four novels, including *Blame* and *Off Course*. She is a senior fiction editor at the *Los Angeles Review of Books*, teaches creative writing at UCLA, and lives in Altadena, California, with her husband, dog, cat, and African grey parrot.

LAURA KIPNIS's latest book is *Men: Notes from an Ongoing Investigation*; her previous books include *How to Become a Scandal*, *The Female Thing*, and *Against Love*. She's a professor in the Radio/TV/Film department at Northwestern, where she teaches filmmaking. She lives in New York and Chicago.

TIM KREIDER, an essayist and cartoonist, is the author of the books *We Learn Nothing*, *Twilight of the Assholes*, *Why Do They Kill Me?*, and *The Pain—When Will It End?* He is a frequent contributor to *The New York Times*, newyorker.com, Al Jazeera, and *Men's Journal*. He lives in New York City and in an undisclosed location on the Chesapeake Bay. His forthcoming book, *I Wrote This Book Because I Love You*, will be published by Simon & Schuster in 2015.

PAUL LISICKY is the author of *Lawnboy*, *Famous Builder*, *The Burning House*, and *Unbuilt Projects*. His awards include fellowships from the National Endowment for the Arts, the James Michener/Copernicus Society, and the Fine Arts Work Center in Provincetown. He has worked as a landscaper, a musician, a salesperson in a clothing store, and a professor of creative writing. He currently teaches in the MFA Program at Rutgers–Camden and divides his time among Philadelphia, Miami, and Provincetown. A memoir, *The Narrow Door*, is forthcoming in late 2015.

M. G. LORD is the author of *The Accidental Feminist: How Elizabeth Taylor Raised Our Consciousness and We Were Too Distracted by Her Beauty to Notice*, *Forever Barbie: The Unauthorized Biography of a Real Doll*, and *Astro Turf*, a family memoir of aerospace culture during the Cold War. She currently lives in Los Angeles and teaches at the University of Southern California. After graduating from Yale, she served for twelve years as the editorial-page cartoonist for *Newsday*. Recently, she again took up her drawing pen to create a graphic novel set in what she considers a perfect world. It is populated exclusively by anthropomorphic animals.

ROSEMARY MAHONEY is the author of six books of nonfiction, including *Down the Nile, Alone in a Fisherman's Skiff*, *A Likely Story: One Summer with Lillian Hellman*, and *For the Benefit of Those Who See: Dispatches from the World of the Blind*. She was educated at Harvard College and the Johns Hopkins University and is the recipient of a 2011 Guggenheim Fellowship, a grant from the National Endowment for the Arts, a Whiting Writers' Award, a nomination for the National Book Critics Circle Award, a Transatlantic Review Award, and Harvard's Charles E. Horman Prize for writing. She has written for numerous publications, including *The New York Times*, *The Wall Street Journal*, *The London Observer*, *The Washington Post Book World*, *The New York Times Sunday Book Review*, and *The New York Times Magazine*. She lives in Rhode Island.

SIGRID NUNEZ has published six novels, including *A Feather on the Breath of God*, *The Last of Her Kind*, and *Salvation City*. She is also the author of *Sempre Susan: A Memoir of Susan Sontag*.

JEANNE SAFER has been a psychoanalyst for forty years. She is author of five books on "taboo topics"—the things everybody thinks but nobody talks about: *Beyond Motherhood: Choosing a Life Without Children*; *Forgiving and Not Forgiving: Why Sometimes It's Better NOT to Forgive*; *The Normal One: Life with a Difficult or Damaged Sibling*; *Death Benefits: How Losing a Parent Can Change an Adult's Life—for the Better*; and *Cain's Legacy: Liberating Siblings from a Lifetime of Rage, Shame, Secrecy, and Regret*. She lives in New York City with her husband, historian and political journalist Richard Brookhiser, and is currently at work on a book about the nature of love, from unrequited to fulfilled.

LIONEL SHRIVER is a prolific journalist and the author of eleven novels, including the best sellers *So Much for That*, *The Post-Birthday World*, and the Orange Prize winner *We Need to Talk About Kevin*, adapted for a feature film in 2011. Her most recent novel, *Big Brother* (2013), addresses obesity. Her work has been translated into twenty-eight languages.